Yosemite

A Guide to Yosemite National Park
California

Produced by the
Division of Publications
National Park Service

U.S. Department of the Interior
Washington, D.C.

Using this Handbook

Yosemite National Park embraces one of the world's most outstanding concentrations of spectacular mountain-and-valley scenery. Its Sierran setting harbors a grand collection of high waterfalls and forests that include groves of giant sequoias, the world's largest living things. Part 1 of this handbook briefly introduces the park and its early conservationist champion, John Muir. Part 2 explores the park's natural and cultural history. Part 3 presents concise travel guide and reference materials, including a full-color map of the park.

National Park Handbooks are published to support the National Park Service's management programs and to promote understanding and enjoyment of the more than 350 National Park System sites, which represent important examples of our country's natural and cultural inheritance. Each handbook is intended to be informative reading and a useful guide before, during, and after a park visit. More than 100 titles are in print. They are sold at parks and can be purchased by mail from the Superintendent of Documents, U.S. Government Printing Office, Washington, DC 20402.

Part 1

Welcome to Yosemite

For You Will Be Mostly in Eternity

"I invite you to join me," John Muir wrote to the eminent Ralph Waldo Emerson in 1871, "in a month's workshop with Nature in the high temples of the great Sierra Crown beyond our holy Yosemite. It will cost you nothing save the time and very little of that, for you will be mostly in Eternity." Muir, the pioneering conservationist and naturalist, had gravitated to Yosemite in 1868 as a sheepherder and stayed on as sawyer and jack-of-all-trades for Yosemite Valley innkeeper and guide James Mason Hutchings. John Muir and Yosemite: It was love at first sight, and the energy appeared to be mutual. Muir enjoyed a spiritual fusion and personal identity with Yosemite. "No temple made with hands can compare with Yosemite. Every rock in its walls seems to glow with life. Some lean back in majestic repose; others, absolutely sheer or nearly so for thousands of feet, advance beyond their companions in thoughtful attitudes, giving welcome to storms and calms alike, seemingly conscious, yet heedless of everything going on about them. Awful in stern, immovable majesty, how softly these mountain rocks are adorned and how fine and reassuring the company they keep." Life, personality, consciousness—Muir found these qualities in what most perceived as inanimate nature. "You'll find me rough as the rocks," he wrote to a friend, "and about the same color—granite."

Nor did Yosemite disappoint Emerson: "This valley is the only place that comes up to the brag about it, and exceeds it," he said. The philosopher's journal haltingly records: "In Yosemite, grandeur of these mountains perhaps unmatched in the globe; for here they strip themselves like athletes for exhibition and stand perpendicular granite walls, showing their entire height, and wearing a liberty cap of snow on the head." Emerson's admiration must have pleased Muir, whose life seemed predicated on the eastern sage's dictum: "We must trust the perfection of the creation so far as to believe that whatever curiosity the order of things has awakened in our minds, the order of things can satisfy."

Behind the intrepid John Muir at this time in his life lay his solo walk of 1,000 miles from Indiana to the Gulf of Mexico. Behind lay his abandoned career as an inventor, his brief studies at the University of Wisconsin, and his Wisconsin farm boyhood. To acquaintances, to family, and even to supportive close friends, this loomed as a formless period for Muir, indeed for all of society in that day. Religion and science faced a new and jarring parting of the ways. The rise of evolutionary theory and the ascendence of new geological theories battered the centuries-old religious paradigm, particularly in universities and the professions. Suddenly, no one knew quite how to view the world.

John Muir was, in fact, finding out how to view it. If his long-distance wanderings, and then his Yosemite forays, seemed formless, they were nonetheless formative. More than a search for knowledge, Muir's was a vision quest; he was developing his "glacial eye" as he called it. The Sierra peaks, Muir realized, were mountain fountains, watering first the "Incomparable Valley" of Yosemite and then the agricultural plenitude of California's Central Valley. Muir envisioned the Central Valley as a "solar gold" lake flowing out of Sierran springs and seeps. The giant sequoias, with sponge-like root systems, similarly held precious water for timed release as the lifeblood of California's agriculture.

Muir's was an early and profoundly influential ecological vision. He saw the universe as flow. Although he published statements of this perspective 15 years before similar statements appeared in scientific literature, Muir has not received proper credit for them. Perhaps the experiences he described in his articles were judged too intensely personal to embody scientific theory.

A Yosemite Panorama

The scenic magnificence of Yosemite Valley in its Sierran setting is dramatically depicted in this panorama by Heinrich Berann of Lans, Austria. From a vantage point above the range's western foothills you are looking eastward up Yosemite Valley to the crest of the High Sierra.

A poster version of this panorama is available from the Yosemite Association at the address shown on page 130.

Panorama Key

1	Matterhorn Peak	7	Mount Watkins	14	Mount Clark
2	Mount Hoffmann	8	Clouds Rest	15	Glacier Point
3	Tioga Pass	9	Mount Maclure	16	Sentinel Dome
4	Mount Dana	10	Mount Lyell	17	Wilma Lake
5	Mount Gibbs	11	Mount Florence	18	Lake Vernon
6	Cathedral Peak	12	Banner Peak	19	Laurel Lake
		13	Mount Ritter		

Illness had thwarted Muir's original plan to travel on southward after his 1,000-mile walk, on to Cuba and South America and the Amazon River's source. Muir went west instead, by steamer. He had left the university with walls for what he called the "University of the Wilderness." Ending up in California, Muir soon spied, walling the eastern horizon, the Sierra Nevada, the mountains he would re-christen "The Range of Light." His Sierran experiences would gain him mythological stature as "John of the Mountains."

"Mr. Muir gazes and gazes, and cannot get his fill . . . . ," Professor Joseph LeConte, a University of California geologist, wrote of this indefatigable mountaineer. "Plants and flowers and forests, and sky and clouds and mountains seem actually to haunt his imagination. He seems to revel in the freedom of this life. I think he would pine away in a city or in conventional life of any kind." LeConte, a respected natural scientist and religious apologist for the new evolutionary viewpoint, found Muir's situation an oddity: "A man of so much intelligence tending a sawmill!—not for himself, but for Mr. Hutchings. This is California!"

Yosemite historian Margaret Sanborn wrote of Muir: "No one has made a more intensive, prolonged, and reverent study of Yosemite Valley and the high country than John Muir. No one understood it better. Nothing was too insignificant for notation; nothing overlooked: a grasshopper's trail in the dust; the lisp of a snowflake alighting; fern fronds uncoiling; the distant calls of Canada geese winging high above the valley on winter nights; the silence following each big storm; the lunar bows in Yosemite Falls at full moon; the night shadows of trees and rocks cast by Venus' light."

Late in his life Muir characterized his early wanderings by describing himself during that time as a "self-styled poetico-trampo-geologist-bot. and ornithnatural, etc!!!" His fateful change in itinerary—California instead of Cuba—eventually sparked new life in him, helped lead to the creation of Yosemite National Park, and helped crystallize for America and the world the national park concept. But if this "John of the Mountains" possessed vision, it was the concrete facts and details of natural history he commanded, as well as the emotions his experiences stirred, that propelled his advocacy for the emergent conservation cause into people's minds and hearts. His advocacy for conservation is still so propelled today. Facts and feelings about nature were John Muir's stock in trade. He relentlessly ferreted out the facts and probed his feelings while wandering and pondering "our holy Yosemite."

"The real voyage of discovery," wrote Marcel Proust, "consists not in seeking new landscapes but in having new eyes." Yosemite Valley's first entry by non-Indian people in 1851 occurred when America possessed new eyes for wildness and the sublime. Fear and antagonism toward wild nature had marked Western attitudes in the preceding centuries, but a reaction of love and respect for nature had begun to appear in American arts and letters by the 1830s.

Muir's hearty invitation to Emerson, couched in religious metaphor, accents this cultural shift. A young doctor serving with the Mariposa Battalion, the first non-Indian people to enter Yosemite Valley, recalled his experience: "The grandeur of the scene was but softened by the haze that hung over the valley—light as gossamer—and by the clouds which partially dimmed the higher cliffs and mountains," wrote Lafayette Bunnell. "This obscurity of vision but increased the awe with which I beheld it, and as I looked, a peculiar exalted sensation seemed to fill my whole being, and I found my eyes in tears with emotion." Popular travel writer the Reverend Thomas Starr King declared in 1860: "Great is granite, and the Yo-Semite is its prophet!"

Centuries earlier some believed Satan lurked in such ragged terrain as the Sierra Nevada. The proper emotion would have been fear and the proper attitude disgust. Beauty inhabited only those things exhibiting order and proportion. Yet Starr King returned to his congregation and preached three Yosemite sermons.

Looking down into the Valley from Old Inspiration Point, writer Fitz Hugh Ludlow, traveling with painter Albert Bierstadt in 1863, summed up the new view of nature: "We did not so much seem to be seeing from the crag of vision a new scene on the old familiar globe as a new heaven and a new earth into which the creative spirit had just been breathed. I hesitate now, as I did then, at the attempt to give my vision utterance. Never were words as beggared for

Next pages: *Bearing autumn's leafy burden, the Merced River beckons you deeper into Yosemite Valley. El Capitan, solid and eternal at left, and Bridalveil Fall, gossamer and ephemeral, seem to stand as its contrasting gatekeepers.*

El Capitan reposes in warm evening light that invests it with illusory softness. "The Chief" challenges rock climbers from around the globe.

In 1855, Thomas A. Ayres drew Yosemite Falls, **opposite,** *picturing the Valley's wonders for a wide public for the first time. This lithograph was made from Ayres' drawing. Yosemite enthusiast James Mason Hutchings, a magazine publisher, included Ayres in the first sightseeing trip to the Valley.*

Left: *Sightseers still seek out scenic Yosemite Falls in all its moods and seasons. The combined height of these falls of Yosemite Creek is 2,425 feet. The Tioga Road crosses the creek between White Wolf and Porcupine Flat with no hint of the falls downstream.*

Long descents and windy conditions render misty and veil-like many Sierran waterfalls. The slow shutter speed used here to capture Bridalveil Creek below Bridalveil Fall exaggerates this lacy, hazy quality. Indians called the waterfall, which plunges 620 feet, Pohono, "powerful wind."

an abridged translation of any Scripture of Nature."

This fundamental about-face in thinking gave rise to the possibility of a national park concept in the United States in the 19th century. But credit for its *probability* goes to the fortuitous combination of John Muir and Yosemite.

Today's social historians describe this shift in attitude toward nature as a reaction to urbanization and industrialization. Also, the seemingly boundless American frontier was visibly closing. Once seemingly limitless, beaver and buffalo were headed toward extirpation throughout the North American vastness. "For land-starved Europeans the New World was a candy store with no lock on the door," environmental historian Roderick Nash wrote. "Environmental responsibility was the last thing on their minds as they faced the setting sun." But the end of the frontier hinted to a chastened America that the candy store could be emptied after all.

Whatever the motivation, by 1851 Henry Thoreau, whose writings would deeply influence Muir, was championing wildness at the Concord Lyceum. In an 1858 *Atlantic Monthly* Thoreau asked: "Why should not we ... have our national preserves ... in which the bear and panther, and some even of the hunter race, may still exist, and not be 'civilized off the face of the earth' ... for inspiration and our true recreation? Or should we, like villains, grub them all up for poaching on our own national domains?" Emerson, James Fenimore Cooper, and others carried the wild nature theme in literature. Painters Thomas Cole, Asher B. Durand, Thomas Moran, and Albert Bierstadt celebrated it in the visual arts. But a newcomer to the arts, a new medium of expression, would also prove a staunch proponent for wild nature.

The rise of photography afforded a new esthetic tool for advocating preservation of wild nature. The Daguerreotype process was invented in 1839, but it was confined to use in the studio. Photography won its freedom to move into the wilds with development of the collodion wet-plate process in 1851. Once liberated from the studio, it offered the public both art and effective documentation. The wet-plate process boasted further advantage: Multiple prints could be made of an image. For aspiring wilderness photographers, however, it wasn't all that easy. This bulky process demanded that the photographer carry view camera, tripod, large and heavy glass plates, chemicals, and the complete darkroom into the wilderness to take a picture. Early exposure times required from ten minutes to a full hour. Despite such physical demands, Timothy O'Sullivan, Charles Leander Weed, Carleton Watkins, Eadweard Muybridge, William Henry Jackson, and others began to capture photographs of the 19th-century American wilderness. From 1860 to 1880, they produced landscape images that stand today among the world's great artistic accomplishments.

Next pages: *As we travel up Yosemite Valley, Half Dome slips back into view in an early morning's light. Washington Column forms the nearly vertical left shank of this Valley profile. Off the foreground gravel bar the column's rounded cap is reflected in the Merced River.*

Many of these historic images documented Yosemite Valley and its Sierra Nevada environs. Yosemite's first tourist had been James Hutchings, for whom Muir later worked. Publisher of *Hutchings' California Magazine,* he took artist Thomas Ayres with him on his first trip to the Valley in 1855. Ayres' drawings and the magazine lithographs made from them gave the world its first Yosemite pictures.

Charles Weed took the first photograph, of Yosemite Falls, in 1859. Weed, too, traveled with Hutchings, the Valley's fanatical publicist who eventually settled here in 1863. At the 1867 Paris International Exposition, Carleton Watkins exhibited his 17x22-inch mammoth-plate Yosemite views. Along with his eventual competitor, Eadweard Muybridge, and Ansel Adams, Watkins ranks among the all-time great Yosemite artists. Watkins' images had already helped inspire Congress and President Abraham Lincoln to protect for public use Yosemite Valley and the Mariposa Grove of Giant Sequoias in 1864, while the Civil War still raged. But it was Muir's sometimes-bizarre Yosemite wanderings and his reading of the landscape that produced the proof that "you cannot save Yosemite Valley without saving its Sierran fountains." We owe principally to John Muir the scope of today's national park.

In November 1860, subscribers to the *Boston Transcript* newspaper sat in their homes and offices to read: "We were very tired when we dismounted at [Galen] Clark's log hut and canvas dining tent in the glorious forest [at Wawona], thirty miles from Mariposa. Tired in body and in brain,—tired by our seven hours of horseback riding, and by the perpetual feast of floral beauty and sugar-pine magnificence which

Left: *Sentinel Rock juts sky-
ward above the Valley to
7,038 feet in elevation. The
contrast of flower-dappled
meadows of the Valley floor
and Cathedral Rocks in the
distance evokes images of
Chinese landscape painting.*

Next pages: *Walled in and
twice etched on memory's
palette with their Merced
River reflections, willows, al-
ders, and black cottonwoods
stage their annual fall-color
spectacle.*

had delighted eye and heart. But it did not require a long time to restore us. Half an hour's rest under one of the stately firs that tower above the cabin, and a cup of tea with our noon meal, fit for a mandarin . . . put us in good working trim for the afternoon's excursion. We were only five miles from the Mammoth Trees. An easy upland ride of an hour would lead us to the [Mariposa] grove where the vegetable Titans we had so often read about with a wonder tinged with unbelief held their solemn court." This excerpt comes from the fourth of six *Boston Transcript* letters—full-length travel articles—recounting the Yosemite journey of Unitarian preacher Thomas Starr King.

Subscribers saved the series. Just before moving to California from Boston, Starr King wrote a guidebook to New Hampshire's White Mountains that won him great stature in the East as a travel writer. Bits and pieces about Yosemite's spectacular features had circulated for several years, but here at last was an authority on scenery confirming that Yosemite was indeed sublime. Yosemite soon took its place on the map and on the grand western tour. When the transcontinental railroad was completed in 1869, a host of eastern notables journeyed west to Yosemite.

Starr King's prose extolling scenery capitalized on the powerful American pride that had begun to swell in the 19th century. This pride fueled the 1864 federal grant of Yosemite Valley and the Mariposa Big Tree Grove to California as a reserve for "public resort and recreation" and helped spark the national park movement. "The argument was that America needed cultural distinctiveness—something different and distinguished to hold up against the older and richer antiquities of the Old World," wrote Roderick Nash. "Specifically, the New World had a quantity and quality of wilderness that transcended anything abroad."

As it was popularly perceived in the America of the mid- to late 1800s, wilderness *was* scenery—a concept John Muir worked assiduously to broaden and deepen—and the more monumental, the better. Big was beautiful; vertical was wonderful. Could we compare favorably with the Swiss Alps? Did we have dazzling attractions for the world traveler? The early parks, the Yosemite Grant and Yellowstone, were preserved as scenic marvels, not as forest or wildlife

Right: *A fire-scarred sequoia persists in the Tuolumne Grove.*

Pioneering photographer Carleton Watkins labeled this photograph The Grizzly Giant, 1861. *It shows Galen Clark — of normal stature — standing against the giant sequoia of that name. First guardian of the Yosemite Grant, which included the Mariposa Big Tree Grove, Clark built a cabin where the grove museum now stands.*

Next pages: *Granite domes stand above Tenaya Lake as seen from Olmsted Point on the Tioga Road. We're in the highcountry now!*

Left: *Caught in afternoon light, Cathedral Lakes Basin shimmers despite the gathering clouds. The basin lies between the Tioga Road and Cathedral Peak beneath the Cathedral Range. It can be reached on foot from Tuolumne Meadows via the John Muir Trail.*

Iron oxide discolors this glacially polished granite in the Cathedral Lakes Basin. Evidence of the last period of glaciation abounds throughout the park. Glacial striations—grooves gouged into bedrock—show which way the glaciers flowed.

Next pages: *A verdant subalpine meadow is sandwiched between contorted Cathedral Peak and its mirror image.*

reserves. These conservation motives came later. The giant sequoias, Starr King's "vegetable Titans," were simply added monumental bonuses. How could Yosemite miss, with its 3,000-foot-high El Capitan, its singularly colossal domes, its plethora of plunging waterfalls, and its giant sequoia groves?

For John Muir the question was rather, "How can we miss the mark so badly?" Was not nature much more than a collection of scenic wonders and curiosities? Muir found in nature a dynamic flow.

Just as Yosemite Valley was born of flowing glaciers, so, too, its life-giving streams were born high on the mountains springing from snowfields and glaciers. To set aside only Yosemite Valley and the Mariposa Grove, as was done in 1864, was, in Muir's view, futile. In the end neither the parts nor the whole would have integrity. "For the branching can[y]ons and valleys of the basins of the streams that pour into Yosemite are as closely related to it as are the fingers to the palm of the hand—as the branches, foliage, and flowers of a tree to the trunk," Muir explained. "Therefore, very naturally, all the fountain region above Yosemite, with its peaks, can[y]ons, snow fields, glaciers, forests, and streams, should be included in the park to make it an harmonious unit instead of a fragment, great though the fragment be." Muir's Yosemite wanderings had brought him a new vision of nature. As Muir saw it, life itself flowed off the crowns of mountains, in turn giving life to surrounding realms.

To fathom the significance of Muir's realizations, we must understand the cultural context of a century ago. Clouding people's perceptions of nature was the notion that humanity was lord over creation. Muir considered this false doctrine. "The world, we are told, was made especially for man—a presumption not supported by all the facts," he wrote in his *Thousand Mile Walk to the Gulf.* Later he elaborated: "No dogma taught by the present civilization seems to form so insuperable an obstacle in the way of a right understanding of the relations which culture sustains to wildness as that which regards the world as made especially for the uses of man." Far better to acknowledge, Muir thought, that "we all travel the milky way together, trees and men. . . ." Eulogizing a bear he found dead in Yosemite, Muir reflected that

Tuolumne Meadows, with its visitor center and other facilities, is a threshold for a vast portion of the Yosemite wilderness. Such subtle and delicate attractions as paintbrush and elephanthead flowers, combined with the mountain backdrop, make Tuolumne Meadows a place that beckons us to return again and again.

Left: *At Tuolumne Meadows the Dana and Lyell forks of the Tuolumne River come together. Here, lit askance at sunset, the plunging water is channelled through the Grand Canyon of the Tuolumne River below Tuolumne Meadows. Farther downstream, O'Shaughnessy Dam, authorized inside this national park in 1913, backs up these waters as Hetch Hetchy Reservoir. Here, however, the river's wildness is unrestrained.* **Below:** *Bracken ferns adorn a slope with a green belt above the Tuolumne River.*

Next pages: *Seen in panoramic view from atop Medlicott Dome, the Tuolumne River country takes on a more severe demeanor. Pocked rock and rain pools in the foreground express in microcosm the landscape that sweeps away from them.* **Pages 44** *and* **45**: *At Dana Meadows, Mammoth Peak is reflected at early morning in a subalpine pond.*

41

Lower Ottoway Lake, forming part of the headwaters of Illilouette Creek, lies in the Clark Range in the southeasterly reaches of Yosemite's backcountry. Merced Peak, at center, lies just a mile inside the park boundary.

"Bears are made of the same dust as we, breathe the same winds and drink of the same waters. A bear's days are warmed by the same sun, his dwellings are overdomed by the same blue sky, and his life turns and ebbs with heart-pulsings like ours. . . ."

"Muir was not on vacation in the Sierra; he was, rather, learning to inhabit the mountains," biographer Michael P. Cohen wrote. "This activity was his life. He was neither botanist nor geologist, but a whole man in a whole Nature, yearning." Muir himself observed that "No scientific book in the world can tell me how this Yosemite granite is put together or how it has been taken down. Patient observation and constant brooding above the rocks, lying upon them for years as the ice did, is the way to arrive at the truths which are graven so lavishly upon them." Muir discovered an active glacier on Merced Peak in the Sierra in 1871. The then-accepted scientific opinion was that there were no glaciers in the Sierra, and indeed never had been. Not content simply to discover glaciers, Muir characteristically descended into a crevasse of one for a closer look.

Cohen observed that ". . . Muir was reborn as a son of Mother Nature when he returned from the glacial womb. He had acquired a deeper appreciation of his own relationship to the wilderness by living with the agents which shaped it and are still shaping it." Geologists of Muir's day were saying that Yosemite was "the ruins of a bygone geological empire." Not so, Muir could answer now. Active agents had shaped this wilderness—and are shaping it still. Josiah D. Whitney, head of California's State Geological Survey, brushed Muir's views aside as those of "an ignorant sheepherder." Ultimately, however, Whitney could not deny the living glaciers that Muir found.

John Muir's way of seeing—not just what he saw—finally prevailed in that geological controversy. While refined and updated in its particulars, it still stands today. It stands as a part of Yosemite, whose glaciers, mountain crags, waterfalls, stately trees, and cavorting squirrels certainly evoked and nurtured it. As a formative ecological vision, it also stands now as a part of our broad cultural heritage.

ALBERT BIERSTADT

Gates of Yosemite,
circa 1872.

ALBERT BIERSTADT

**Cathedral Rocks, Yosemite
Valley,** *circa 1872.*

EADWEARD MUYBRIDGE

Scene on the Merced River,
1867.

Landscape Photography
*The collodion wet-plate
process liberated the new
art of photography from the
studio in 1851, the year that
Yosemite Valley was first entered by non-Indian people.
The park and landscape photography grew up together,
to great mutual benefit.*

CHARLES WEED

Mirror Lake, *1865.*

JULIUS BOYSEN

Self-Portrait. Boysen is at left,
with his brother and father,
1901.

CARLETON WATKINS

The Half Dome, from Gla-
cier Point, Yosemite, *circa
1878-1881.*

Artist Thomas Moran drew his Glacier on Mount Ritter *from a sketch by the intrepid Yosemite explorer John Muir, shown here as a young man.*

Early History at a Glance

A chronology from 1776 to the establishment of the National Park Service in 1916.

1776   Sierra Nevada named by Padre Pedro Font.

1806   Merced River named when Moraga Expedition explores its lower course.

1833   Joseph Walker party of trappers crosses present park and looks down into Yosemite Valley.

1845   John C. Fremont explores Mariposa foothills and engages in battle with local Indians but does not learn of the existence of Yosemite Valley.

1848   Non-Indians find gold in Sierra Nevada north of Yosemite.

1850   Miners converge on Mariposa area in search for gold. Conflicts between miners and Indians increase. Indians retaliate by attacking James Savage's trading posts. First reported entry of Hetch Hetchy Valley by non-Indians attributed to Nate Screech.

1851   Mariposa Battalion seeks Ahwahneechee Indians and explores and renames Yosemite Valley. Capt. John Boling's company re-enters Valley, captures Chief Tenaya's band, and removes them to Fresno River Reservation. They are permitted to return to Valley in winter.

1852   Prospectors enter Valley. Two are killed, allegedly by Indians. Troops under Lt. Tredwell Moore execute six Indian men. Indians seek refuge with Mono Indians at Mono Lake. Moore finds promising mineral deposits east of Sierra crest.

1853   Chief Tenaya killed in dispute with Mono Lake Paiute Indians. Many prospectors enter Valley.

1854   James Capen Adams visits Yosemite to capture grizzlies. As "Grizzly Adams" he trains them for show.

1855   James Mason Hutchings brings first party of sightseers to Yosemite. First sketches of Yosemite made by Thomas Ayres. Trail built from South Fork (Wawona) to Yosemite Valley. Galen Clark engaged to survey for water supply to Mariposa Fremont grant. Surveyors build first house, a roofless shack, in Valley.

1856   Coulterville Free Trail completed. Ayres returns to make more drawings. Lower Hotel built by Walworth and Hite at base of Sentinel Rock.

1857   Rush of miners from Tuolumne over Mono Trail to Mono Diggings. Canvas-covered house constructed in Valley on site of Cedar Cottage. Galen Clark settles at Wawona and explores Mariposa Grove.

1858   Upper Hotel (later named Cedar Cottage) built. Cogswell party visits Tuolumne Grove of Big Trees.

1859   Charles L. Weed makes first photograph in Yosemite. James C. Lamon takes up summer residence in Valley.

1861   Pioneering photographer Carleton E. Watkins visits Yosemite.

1863   California State Geological Survey makes expedition to region between Upper Merced and Tuolumne Rivers. Painter Albert Bierstadt makes first visit to Yosemite.

1864 Hutchings takes over Upper Hotel and renames it Hutchings House. Birth of Florence Hutchings, first white child born in Yosemite. Yosemite Valley and Mariposa Big Tree Grove granted to California as public trust. Board of Commissioners created with Frederick Law Olmsted as chairman.

1868 John Muir arrives in Yosemite for first time.

1869 Leidig's and Black's hotels built. Peregoy's Mountain View House built near Bridalveil Creek. Transcontinental Railroad completed with extension from Sacramento to Stockton.

LEIDIG'S HOTEL, YO SEMITE VALLEY.
ALWAYS OPEN and no pains spared to accommodate and please.

Mrs. G. F. LEIDIG, Proprietress.

SENTINEL ROCK 3,270 Ft. SENTINEL FALLS 3,200 Ft.
YO SEMITE FALLS 2,634 Ft. directly in front.

Zith Crocker & Co. S.F.

1870 Albert Snow builds trail to flats between Vernal and Nevada falls and builds La Casa Nevada. Geology professor Joseph LeConte visits Yosemite for first time. John Muir explores Grand Canyon of the Tuolumne River. J.C. Smith builds Cosmopolitan Bathhouse and Saloon in Valley.

1871 Ascent of Half Dome attempted. Four-Mile Trail from Valley to Glacier Point begun by John Conway. Mount Lyell climbed by J.B. Tileston.

1872 Central Pacific Railroad reaches Merced. Stage road built on north side of Yosemite Valley. Great Inyo earthquake occurs. Telegraph lines extend into Valley.

1873 Eagle Peak Trail built to foot of Upper Yosemite Fall.

1874 Coulterville and Big Oak Flat roads built to Valley floor. Road built from "Hutchings'" up south side of Valley. Private claims in Yosemite Valley purchased by State of California.

1875 Wawona Road completed to Valley floor. Half Dome climbed by George Anderson. Wawona Hotel purchased by Washburn brothers from Galen Clark and partner Edwin Moore.

1876 Sentinel Hotel built in Valley. Mountain House built at Glacier Point. Muir publishes first article on devastation of High Sierra meadows by domestic sheep grazing.

1878 John L. Murphy settles at Tenaya Lake. Highcountry surveyed. First public campgrounds established in Valley. Tunnel cut in Tuolumne Grove's Dead Giant.

57

1879   Yosemite Chapel constructed in Valley.

1880   Legislature ousts Board of Yosemite Commissioners. Hutchings appointed guardian. Account of Valley's discovery published by L. H. Bunnell.

1881   Washburn brothers pay Scribner brothers $75 to cut tunnel through Mariposa Grove's Wawona Tree.

1882   "Anderson Trail" built from Happy Isles toward bridge below Vernal Fall. Great Sierra Wagon (Tioga) Road construction begins. Road built to Glacier Point by John Conway.

1883   Former President Rutherford B. Hayes and party visit Yosemite Valley. Great Sierra Wagon Road completed.

1884   Mr. and Mrs. John Degnan establish bakery and store, Yosemite's oldest concession. Hutchings removed as guardian; W. E. Dennison appointed.

1885   Tuolumne Meadows homesteaded by John B. Lembert. Panorama Trail built from Nevada Fall to Glacier Point. Log Cabin built in Mariposa Grove.

1886   John L. Murphy homesteads 160 acres at Tenaya Lake.

1888   Commissioners remove Black's and Leidig's hotels. J. J. Cook leases newly built Stoneman House.

1889   Galen Clark appointed guardian again. Mirror Lake dammed to enlarge it.

1890   Yosemite National Park created; Muir's writings influential in movement to designate it a national park.

1891   U.S. Cavalry arrives to administer and protect national park with headquarters in Wawona. First telephones installed in Yosemite Valley.

1892   Sierra Club formed, with Muir as president, to secure federal protection for entire Yosemite region. First trout planted in Yosemite by California Fish and Game Commission.

1893   Sierra Forest Reservation created.

1895   Fish hatchery established at Wawona.

1896   Stoneman House destroyed by fire.

1897   Wooden ladders at Vernal Fall replaced by rock steps.

1898	Archie O. Leonard named first civilian park ranger.
1899	Curry Camping Company established by David and Jenny Curry. Artist Chris Jorgensen establishes studio in Valley.

1900	Oliver Lippincott drives first car into Yosemite.

1901	Sierra Club holds first of its annual outings at Tuolumne Meadows.
1902	Artist Harry Cassie Best establishes studio (now doing business as Ansel Adams Gallery). Pioneer innkeeper James Mason Hutchings dies in carriage accident.
1903	Sierra Club builds LeConte Memorial Lodge in Valley. U.S. Weather Bureau installs instruments in Yosemite. President Theodore Roosevelt meets John Muir in Yosemite.

1905	Park reduced in size. California recedes Valley and Mariposa Big Tree Grove to United States.
1906	Congress accepts the recession of Valley and Mariposa Grove to federal jurisdiction. Superintendent's headquarters moved from the Wawona area to Yosemite Valley.
1907	Yosemite Valley Railroad opened from Merced to El Portal. Extensive telephone system installed in park.
1908	Hetch Hetchy rights granted to City of San Francisco. Pacific Telephone and Telegraph Co. builds telephone line from El Portal to Sentinel Hotel.
1910	Galen Clark dies at 96.
1912	Sierra Club purchases Soda Springs property at Tuolumne Meadows.
1913	Automobiles admitted to Yosemite Valley. Raker Act authorizes damming and inundation of Hetch Hetchy Valley as reservoir.
1914	John Muir dies at age 76 on Christmas Eve. Civilian employees replace military in administration of Yosemite.
1915	Yosemite Lodge established. Stephen T. Mather purchases Tioga Road and gives it to federal government. Motor stages replace horse-drawn stages.
1916	Congress establishes National Park Service. Stephen T. Mather appointed Director. W.B. Lewis named Superintendent of Yosemite National Park.

Part 2

Dark Forests and Shining Rocks

Scenery, and a
New Way of Seeing

El Capitan, looming at left here, is perhaps the world's largest exposed granite monolith—twice the height of the Rock of Gibraltar. The cliff rises 3,000 feet from the Valley floor and the summit is almost 600 feet higher. What Half Dome, at right, may lack in mass, it makes up for in its sculpture.

Yosemite struck John Muir as the "sanctum sanctorum of the Sierra" and "the grandest of all the special temples of Nature." Art historian David Robertson recently speculated that Yosemite Valley may be the "global masterpiece" of those awesome artists "Volcano, Earthquake, Glacier, Wind, and Water." The secret of its impact—whether remarked in the religious terms of Muir's day or the geophysical terms of our day—surely lies with the harmonious scenic beauty of its grand vistas.

"I sit in a kind of delicious dream, the scenery unconsciously mingling with my dream," Joseph LeConte, University of California geology professor, confided in his Yosemite trip journal. "I have heard and read much of this wonderful valley, but I can truly say I have never imagined the grandeur of the reality." John Muir felt that in Yosemite Valley "Nature had gathered her choicest treasures" into this one mountain mansion. "No temple made with hands can compare with Yosemite," he propounded. "Every rock in its walls seems to glow with life."

Streams of visual artists have also attested to its beauty since the wider world first heard of this incomparable Sierran valley. Its immensity and grandeur sparked the public imagination. Here are colossal sculptured rockforms, a stupendous collection of waterfalls, and, embracing all, serene majesty. Artists have long sensed the especially evocative spiritual and emotional qualities of this national park. Their sense has not been lost on the rest of us, pilgrims from around the globe responding to Yosemite's allure.

But how did glacier, wind, water, and even volcanic eruption and earthquake sculpt their admitted global masterpiece?

Arising shortly after Yosemite Valley's discovery by non-Indian people, this question proved difficult to answer. We like to think that if it were first posed today we could readily research it and reach consensus. Perhaps, but certainly not so in the second half of the 19th century. The question of the valley's origin caused many minds—and professional egos—to collide in often rancorous controversy for 70 years. Why did this Valley only seven miles long and variably a mile wide set the stage for seven decades of scientific skirmishing?

Josiah D. Whitney, director of the California State Geological Survey, and John Muir were the chief antagonists in this conflict. In *The Yosemite Guide-Book*, Whitney branded John Muir "an ignoramus" and "mere sheepherder" for his views. Geologist Clarence King, then a Whitney associate, publicly characterized Muir as an "ambitious amateur" in danger of "hopelessly floundering" and deluding real geologists who had not inspected the terrain.

Shifting cultural values marking that era decidedly complicated the Yosemite controversy. Religious doctrine about landscape origins ran a collision course with the upstart science of geology, whose own entrenched dogma drew fire from scientists beginning to accept the concepts of evolutionary change and processes. These concepts included the novel theory of glaciation, which Muir championed as the key to how Yosemite Valley came to be.

Swiss scientist Louis Agassiz formulated the theory that the world's northerly latitudes were significantly shaped by episodes of extensive glaciation. Agassiz first tracked the evidence in the Swiss Alps. With the benefit of hindsight we now know that such evidence is not difficult to find. The difficulty then lay in knowing what to look for. Geologists before Agassiz had searched for evidence of the cataclysmic Biblical flood. Muir's intimate ramblings in the High Sierra wilderness introduced him to abundant glacial polish, striations, and erratic boulders. Finally he found actual glaciers near the Sierra's crest. Muir theorized that these were remnants of massive rivers of ice that had once gouged out Yosemite Valley and sculptured its stately granite monuments.

In 1913, respected Dutch-born geologist François E. Matthes commenced a study that devoted 17 years to the question of Yosemite Valley's origins. Employed by the U.S. Geological Survey and urged on by the Sierra Club, Matthes began by studying a larger section of the Sierra. His "Geologic History of the Yosemite Valley" saw print in 1930 and still serves today as the basis for interpreting the Valley's origins. Matthes' report vindicated Muir's hypothesis of glacial formation but rectified many details. Muir, who had died in 1914, had been correct in theory, but he had overstated its application. The Sierra Nevada, Muir had concluded, "may be regarded as one grand wrinkled sheet of glacial records. . . ."

Muir's credibility took a quantum leap with his discovery of an active glacier on Merced Peak in 1871. If residual glaciers were still active in the Sierra, then massive predecessors could have performed colossal work here, he speculated. Even Agassiz extolled Muir's glacier studies: "Here is the first man who has any adequate conception of glacial action."

Certainly Muir's success lay partly in his methods, which are legendary if not mythic: "No scientific book in the world can tell me how this Yosemite granite is put together or how it has been taken down. Patient observation and constant brooding above the rocks, lying upon them for years as the ice did, is the way to arrive at the truths which are graven so lavishly upon them." Muir entered the lives of the glaciers. He described himself moving over rocks like a glacier, in a kind of mystical communion with the Sierra's history. "You'll find me rough as the rocks," he wrote to a friend, "and about the same color—granite."

Michael Cohen placed Muir in the era of the great western American surveys during the period 1860 to 1890. Team expeditions were mounted by Ferdinand Hayden, John Wesley Powell, King, Whitney, and others. "He confronted alone," Cohen said of Muir, "the same wilderness that the giants of western exploration faced with large expeditionary teams." Muir's methods were totally different from the expeditioners'. "They brought the city into the wilderness . . . ," Cohen wrote. "He followed his wild body into the wilderness." Whereas the nature of an expedition meant that it would likely be predetermined by the civilization sending it out, "Muir's way allowed him to reevaluate his mission constantly."

As we understand the Sierra's geological story now, the area that was to become the present range was once covered by water at the western margin of

Against contemporary ortho-doxy, John Muir championed the new theory of glaciation to explain Yosemite Valley's geologic evolution. Muir, **facing page,** *soon elicited the ire of California State Geologist Josiah D. Whitney, pictured at the left with Charles F. Hoffmann and Clarence King, fellow members of the state's geological survey, in 1863.*

Evolution of the Valley

The area that was to become the Sierra Nevada once lay beneath a sea at the west margin of North America. The rock that was formed on this sea floor from deposited silt, mud, and marine organisms was subsequently lifted above sea level and flexed into a mountain range surmounted by a chain of volcanoes much like today's Cascade Range. Granite that formed from molten rock at the roots of these volcanoes eventually would remain as the core of the Sierra Nevada after the overlying sedimentary and volcanic rock gradually weathered and eroded away.

① 50 million years ago. The landscape consisted of rolling hills, broad valleys, and meandering streams. The Merced River meandered through a wide trough whose slopes supported hardwood forests.

② 10 million years ago. A more dissected landscape ensued as the whole range was uplifted and tilted westward. This westward tilt accelerated the Merced River's flow and the river cut deeper into its valley. The climate grew cooler and drier. Forests of coniferous trees, including sequoias, dominated.

③ 3 million years ago. A canyon landscape developed with continued uplift. The raging Merced cut its canyon as much as 3,000 feet deep. Its tributary streams, with smaller drainage basins and volumes of water, cut more slowly. The Ice Age's approach brought a colder climate and thinning forests.

④ 1 million to 250,000 years ago. At least one and perhaps more glacial advances filled Yosemite Valley to its brim. Half Dome projected 900 feet above the ice, but many

66

peaks to the north were engulfed. The Valley was gouged and quarried into a U-shaped trough with steep walls. Many Merced River tributaries were now cascades high above the Valley.

5 **30,000 years ago.** During the Tioga glaciation Yosemite Glacier, a smaller ice sheet, advanced into the Valley and terminated near Bridalveil Fall. As thin as it was, it had little erosive power to enlarge the Valley further.

6 **10,000 years ago.** The last Valley glacier has melted and its terminal moraine has dammed the Valley to create a shallow lake, Lake Yosemite. This was only the last of many Lake Yosemites that probably followed each glaciation. The deep excavation created by earlier glaciers, as much as 2,000 feet into bedrock beneath the present floor of Yosemite Valley,

was already filled with glacial till and sediments long before the Tioga glaciation. This last advance of ice had insufficient erosive power to reexcavate the Valley to any appreciable depth. Lake Yosemite eventually filled in with silt, leaving today's level Valley floor. The photograph shows Mirror Lake. Today it is filling in through the same natural processes. Glaciers did not directly create today's free-leaping waterfalls, although they helped set the stage. The falls plunge into alcoves in the Valley walls, produced by frost-splitting of rock fragments off the lower parts of the cliffs over which the waterfalls formerly cascaded. Where the cliffs are dry most of the time, frost action is not so effective.

Highest level of glaciation 7000ft

El Capitan

Pre-glacial valley profile

Cathedral Rocks

4600ft

Present valley floor 3900ft

Sediments

U-shaped valley profile

BEDROCK

67

Boldly Sculptured Granite

Dome Formation. Many domes are visible from Glacier Point, above Yosemite Valley (see map on page 124). Half Dome, Sentinel Dome, the Starr King group (inset), and many others have been formed by exfoliation. *To exfoliate* means to cast off in scales, plates, or sheets—the spalling off of rock layers on otherwise un-jointed granite. Exfoliation is caused by outward expansion of the granite. This occurs as a result of load relief—when the overburden that once capped the granite has eroded away. The tendency of the fractures formed during exfoli-ation to cut corners is what ultimately results in rounded dome-like forms even though the starting shape may have been angular. Liberty Cap, Fairview Dome, and Lembert Dome are *roches mouton-nées*—elongate rounded rocks sculptured by ice—formed as glacial ice overrode exfoliating granite outcroppings.

Starr King Group from the S.W.

Illustrating Dome forms and combinations

The arrows indicate the direction of the overswelping ice current

Half Dome. Domes are rare in nature, half domes more so. Was Half Dome ever whole? What happened? The impression one has from the Valley that this is a round dome that has lost its northwest half is incorrect. The truth is apparent when you see Half Dome from Glacier Point. It is actually a thin ridge of rock oriented N.E.-S.W., with its southeast side almost as steep as its northwest side, except for the very top. Probably 80 percent of the original northwest portion is still there. What probably happened is that frost-splitting of the rock at the back of a tiny glacier against Half Dome above Mirror Lake gradually quarried the base of the steep northwest face, undermining the upper portion that then fell away. Ultimately parts of the sheets parallel to the original surface of Half Dome were left projecting outward at the crest of the nearly vertical cliff.

A Grand Collection of Waterfalls

Yosemite Falls. Upper Yosemite Fall (1,430 feet), Lower Yosemite Fall (320 feet), and intermediate cascades (675 feet) combine for a height of 2,425 feet. John Muir likened the Upper Fall's force to "a throng of comets."

Vernal Fall. The Merced River plunges 317 feet for its last great fling before it reaches the Valley, spreading in a broad sheet up to 80 feet wide. Its mist creates spectacular arched rainbows at its base during spring runoff.

Bridalveil Fall. The fall drops 620 feet into an alcove from a hanging valley just below Cathedral Rocks, which buttress Yosemite Valley directly opposite El Capitan. Bridalveil Fall is often blown into the filmy mist that suggested the present name.

Nevada Fall. The mighty Sierra cataract plunges the Merced River 594 feet downward, making it look like a thundering snow avalanche. Seen from Glacier Point, Vernal and Nevada falls are like set pieces on what is known as the Giant's Stairway.

North America. Accumulating sediments deposited on the sea floor built up thick layers of rock. Crustal forces, essentially intense heat and pressure, warped these rock strata, lifted them above sea level, and flexed them into a folded mountain range. During this time molten rock welled up from within the Earth, then slowly cooled and crystallized beneath the sea-born rock, as well as forming volcanoes on the Earth's surface much like today's Cascade Range. This embryonic granite became exposed after the sedimentary and volcanic overburden gradually eroded away. This relatively gentle landscape underwent subsequent uplift and westward tilt that steepened the western slope and intensified the erosive power of major westward-flowing streams, which cut V-shaped canyons as much as 2,000 feet deep. Finally the upwarping land mass cracked along the present Sierran crest and the land to the east was left behind as the range continued to rise, creating the steep eastern escarpment.

The great Ice Age saw glaciers advance from the crest at least 10 times in the past two million years. Where the granite was jointed and cracked, glaciers quarried and carried away great blocks. Where the granite was solid, the glaciers could only scrape, buff, and polish. Glaciers ground, gouged, and excavated the canyons wider and deeper as U-shaped troughs, at the same time removing the lower sections of tributary stream channels that intersected the major canyons. The carving action of the glaciers that moved through the troughs of the Merced and Tuolumne canyons left the side canyons as hanging valleys and their streams as plunging waterfalls. Many of Yosemite's domes also were accentuated at this time, as ice overrode exfoliating granite outcroppings and removed remnants of broken outer layers or shells.

Muir's stature as naturalist and writer derives staying power from *what* he sought on his forays into the Sierran wilderness. A clue lies with Muir saying of Yosemite Valley: "Every rock in its walls seems to glow with life." Muir was not looking simply for an origin for the Valley. He sought a new way of seeing nature. Rocks aglow with life suggest a living landscape. Remarkably, this seemed not to be for Muir a metaphor but a statement of fact. Yosemite Valley

Beginning in 1913, geologist François Matthes devoted 17 years of study to the question of Yosemite Valley's formation. He found that Muir's glacial theory was essentially correct, but that Muir had overstated his case. Seismic studies of the Valley in the mid-1930s established its U-shaped profile—characteristic of glaciation—and definitively demolished the theories of Josiah D. Whitney.

was not the ruins of a past creation, as many 19th-century scientists thought. Rather it was an integral part of a living landscape. Yosemite was a wilderness still being shaped by dynamic, constant forces and processes. Discovery of active glaciers confirmed this premise for John Muir.

Muir arrived at this view of nature as dynamic only through great psychic and physical hardship. "I'll acquaint myself with the glaciers and wild gardens, and get as near the heart of the world as I can," he wrote. This represented a painful break with the rigid orthodoxy of his family's deep Christian roots. It also ran counter to the prevailing utilitarian attitude toward nature that repeatedly threatened Yosemite Valley's integrity and led to the tragic damming of the Tuolumne River and the inundation of Hetch Hetchy, Muir's "other Yosemite." Muir's Sierran wanderings often involved great privation and harrowing danger. Yet it is his perspective that we would do well to adopt to assure the preservation of Yosemite and, indeed, the future livability of our beleaguered planet. The rewards are considerable: In a 1908 journal passage, arguing against the utilitarian view of nature, Muir wrote that ". . . the true ownership of the wilderness belongs in the highest degree to those who love it most."

Use of Hetch Hetchy Valley as a reservoir to supply San Francisco with water was approved when President Woodrow Wilson signed into law the Raker Act on December 19, 1913. John Muir, the Sierra Club, and other conservation interests bitterly opposed damming the Tuolumne River (bottom photo) and inundating, in Muir's words, this "other Yosemite." Muir was devastated. A result of this exploitation within a designated national park was the creation of the National Park Service in 1916. In 1938, O'Shaughnessy Dam was raised by 85 feet to its present height.

Sierra Rainshadow

As the mountains force moist, warm eastbound air upward, the air is cooled and is forced increasingly to release moisture as precipitation. By the time it crosses the range, the air has dropped most of its moisture. East of the Sierra Nevada, in its rainshadow, lies the semi-arid Great Basin. On the Sierra's west slope precipitation increases with elevation, generally speaking, to about 8,000 or 9,000 feet, with the maximum precipitation between 5,000 and 8,000 feet. Here is found the most complex and luxuriant forest development. At higher elevations, with less moisture, more intense cold, and stronger winds, tree growth is inhibited. Near treeline only trees such as the whitebark pine can survive the extreme conditions of high elevation. The upper limit of elevation for a tree species may be higher on the Sierra's west slope than on its drier east slope. Annual precipitation at Yosemite's South Entrance (5,120 feet in elevation), on the Sierra's west slope, is 44.9 inches; in Yosemite Valley, 36 inches. At Ellery Lake (9,645 feet in elevation) near Tioga Pass it is 22.85 inches. Most

The illustration shows a generalized progression of forest types on the Sierra's west and east slopes, revealing the effects of the rainshadow.

Subalpine belt
Lodgepole pine, mountain hemlock, western white pine, whitebark pine

Lodgepole pine/red fir belt
Red fir, lodgepole pine, western juniper, western white pine, sugar pine, white fir

6,500 feet

Mixed conifer belt
Ponderosa pine, incense-cedar, black oak, Douglas-fir, white alder, white fir, Jeffrey-pine, sugar pine

3,500 feet

of the park's precipitation falls as snow from November through March. The relatively

dry period from June through August helps make the Sierra Nevada particularly attractive for summer outdoor recreation.

Alpine belt
A few whitebark pine exhibiting krummholz effect, perennial herbs.

Alpine belt
A few whitebark pine, exhibiting krummholz effect, perennial herbs

10,000 feet

Subalpine belt
Whitebark pine, lodgepole pine, mountain hemlock, western juniper, aspen

8,000 feet

7,200 feet
Jeffrey pine belt
Jeffrey pine, aspen

Sagebrush belt
Sagebrush, pinyon pine, mountain mahogany

6,000 feet

For purposes of comparison this diagram exaggerates the topography. Immediately east of Yosemite the lowest elevations are approximately 6,000 feet.

Oak woodland belt
Ponderosa pine, incense-cedar, black oak, canyon live oak

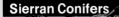

1 On lower slopes of their range, **whitebark pines** grow to 40 feet in height. **2** Large **red firs**, growing to 180 feet in height, often form pure stands, unlike most Sierran forest trees. **3** Tall and large, **sugar pines** grow to 210 feet in height. Their cones average one foot long without stalk. **4** Common in Yosemite Valley, **ponderosa pines**, which are yellow pines, grow to 200 feet in height.

❶ Whitebark pine
Elevation range
10,000 to 12,000 feet

❷ Red fir
Elevation range
6,500 to 9,000 feet

78

3 Sugar pine
Elevation range
4,500 to 7,500 feet

4 Ponderosa pine
Elevation range
3,000 to 6,000 feet

In the Mountains We Find More Than We Seek

Ponderosa pine bark patterns resemble in miniature a relief model of mesa-and-butte landscape forms. Ponderosa pines are common in Yosemite Valley.

"Wherever we go in the mountains, or indeed in any of God's wild fields, we find more than we seek," Muir observed in *My First Summer in the Sierra*. "Descending four thousand feet in a few hours, we enter a new world—climate, plants, sounds, inhabitants, and scenery all new or changed."

Its mountain character indeed provides the essential clue to the biotic richness of Yosemite National Park. More than 230 species of birds, 80 species of mammals, and 1,400 species of classified shrubs, trees, and flowering plants have been recorded in the park. Elevations at El Portal, the floor of Yosemite Valley, and Tioga Pass are approximately 2,000, 4,000, and 10,000 feet, respectively. Above Tioga Pass Mt. Dana tops out at 13,053 feet. Habitat wealth is concentrated vertically. You can, for example, through well-timed upward plodding, make spring last six months in this park whose Tioga Road may be closed as many as eight months of the year by snow. You begin with spring's first lowlands blush, usually in March, and chart its progressively unfolding life through increasingly higher elevations until it expires, late in the summer months, in the spare alpine zone near the summits of the park's high peaks. Chasing spring, you will doubtless appreciate Muir's sense that in the Yosemite wilderness ". . . there is no rectilineal sectioning of times and seasons. All things *flow* here in indivisible, measureless currents."

The mountains also create diversity through their effect on the water cycle. Eastward-moving air masses, laden with moisture from the Pacific, are forced ever higher by the Sierra. As elevation increases, temperatures drop until the clouds must lose their moisture as precipitation. West-slope Sierran forest belts, legacies of this cloud-captive moisture, stand in prodigal contrast to the semi-arid eastern slope and the Mono Basin. Cresting and crossing the range, the air masses have all but spent their life-sustaining moisture. The range divides water wealth—

however unevenly—and so greatly determines who and what in this natural regime lives where.

Life forms tend to occur in zones roughly limited by elevation, moisture, and exposure, making mountain surfaces like biotic layer cakes. At one time these zones were given such names as Upper Sonoran and Arctic-Alpine. Now they are correlated to the dominant plant types in their communities of vegetation. The former Upper Sonoran of the Sierran foothills, for example, is now called the Digger Pine-Chaparral Belt. Arctic-Alpine corresponds to today's Alpine Zone, whose rigors above treeline make it the most uniform of global habitats.

Birds, adept at rapid vertical travel, can exploit a wealth of habitats to sustain themselves. The peregrine falcon is a predatory bird of cliffs and mountain heights, a fabled speedster that dives as fast as 200 miles per hour. Despite its own relatively light weight, the falcon's dive, or stoop, can break the bones of—and knock unconscious—its prey. Grown men have been knocked out by falcons.

The peregrine falcon is an endangered species whose populations have been decimated by pesticide contamination. After an absence of nearly 30 years, an active peregrine falcon nest site, or aerie, was discovered on El Capitan in 1978. At the time, it was the only known site in the entire Sierra Nevada. Organo-chlorine pesticides, especially DDT, were responsible for the near-extinction of peregrine falcons. Populations of the falcons started to rebound after a ban on DDT use was passed in 1972. Gradually, historic aeries in the Sierra Nevada are being reoccupied, including those in Yosemite.

For many years, however, the recovery of peregrine falcons in Yosemite required human assistance. The residual effects of DDT continued to affect falcons as they accumulated residues through the food chain. Such contamination caused female falcons to lay eggs with critically thin shells that broke during incubation or resulted in death of the embryos from desiccation or toxicity. The eggs of females with a history of eggshell thinning were removed from aeries for safe hatching in a laboratory incubator. The eggs were replaced with captive hatched young, which were accepted by the parents.

Manipulations such as this augmenting of falcon nests point up of the difficulties and dilemmas of managing natural systems in today's world. Ideally, natural ecosystems and processes would simply be left alone. But the peregrine falcon's important niche in the natural scheme suffers from continued use of DDT in Latin American countries, where migratory birds that falcons prey upon accumulate DDT residues, and from other pesticides still in use in the United States.

The primary objective of the park's resources management program is to preserve and restore the natural processes that have influenced the development of the park's ecosystems. The restoration of altered systems and the reintroduction of certain species are necessary to achieve this objective. The goal is to restore, to the fullest extent feasible, natural conditions that can be maintained by allowing natural processes to operate largely unimpaired. Fittingly, the National Park Service began aiding the falcon in the same decade that Congress designated 90 percent of the park as wilderness and the park was named a World Heritage Site.

Forests where natural fire has been suppressed for as much as a century may require restoration of more natural conditions. Pristine forests were more open than contemporary forests, with less dead and down wood and fewer trees crowding their understories. Sporadic fires burned frequently enough to preclude such fuel buildup. Fire suppression has created the potential for destructive holocausts, allowing the density and height of the understory to increase. Enough forest litter and undergrowth build up to fuel hot fires that can burn through protective bark and reach the crowns of tall trees.

To correct problems stemming from well-intentioned fire-suppression and to restore natural conditions, the park's resource managers now use prescribed burning. Fires are set to simulate the burning patterns and intensities of natural fires and restore fire's proper ecological role in the natural scheme. Prescribed burns are set only under optimum weather and fuel-moisture conditions. Furthermore, natural fires may be allowed to burn if they do not threaten public safety, historic or archeological resources, buildings and campgrounds, or sensitive resources.

Fire is especially important for perpetuating giant sequoia groves. Long-term ecological studies show

The Mountain World

In subalpine and alpine realms of the mountain world small is beautiful—and most pragmatic. Demanding conditions challenge plant and animal survival: extreme winter temperatures, persistent winds, short growing seasons, thin soils, and exposure to intense sunlight contribute to desert-like conditions. Basic plant adaptations to these harsh conditions include dwarfism, oversized root systems, matting, succulent leaves, and red pigmentation. Some living alpine plants are almost brown rather than green, a feature that protects them from destructive sun rays that the thin atmosphere at high elevations cannot screen out. Dwarfism and matting keep plants low to the ground, where conditions are less severe than just inches higher. Test this yourself by lying down on a mountain pass on a windy day and then sitting up. No wonder nothing stands tall in this mountain realm!

Some alpine flowers are pollinated not by bees but by spiders, whose blood remains liquid at lower temperatures. Highcountry hikers often witness spiders scampering over snowbanks to scavenge the cold-benumbed insects that updrafts waft in from lower elevations. With exceptions such as a grasshopper that cannot fly and the pika's fur-covered feet, animals have adapted to these demanding conditions

Plants and animals of the mountain world:

1 Red-tailed hawk
2 Pika
3 Yellow-bellied marmot

4 Alpine buckwheat
5 Whitebark pine, krummholz
6 Whitebark pine, krummholz
7 White heather
8 Dwarf willow
9 Map lichen

through behavioral rather than structural alteration. Pikas harvest and store hay in late summer and fall for winter consumption. Marmots build body fat in preparation for hibernation. Birds are the most plentiful vertebrate animals here because, by flying, they can readily dip into several ecosystems for food. Prairie falcons and other raptors prey over vast areas from their mountain strongholds. Wary bighorn sheep (inset) were extirpated from their former native range here years ago. An interagency project financed by The Yosemite Fund, a fundraising initiative of the nonprofit Yosemite Association and now a separate organization, restored a population of these mammals to the Yosemite region in 1986.

10 Rosy Finch
11 Alpine forget-me-not
12 Campion or catchfly
13 Spreading phlox
14 Haircap moss

What is the difference between sequoias and redwoods?
The giant sequoia, below, has a column-like trunk; huge, stout branches; and its bark is cinnamon-colored. Its scientific name is Sequoiadendron giganteum. *It is sometimes called the Sierra redwood.*

The taller and more slender coast redwood, Sequoia sem-

that periodic fire creates both the heat and the soil conditions sequoia seeds require for successful germination. Fibrous, thick sequoia bark naturally protects the tree against fires that help ensure propagation of the species. Historic photographs depict these groves as more open than today. Occasional natural wildfires once destroyed the white firs that now crowd the groves' understories and produce shade that sequoia seedlings cannot tolerate.

To rectify another resource deficit, in March 1986, the California Department of Fish and Game, the National Park Service, and the U.S. Forest Service reintroduced California bighorn sheep to their former High Sierra habitat in the vicinity of the park. A relatively large and widespread population of the graceful bighorns once inhabited Yosemite's highcountry, but the animal was declared extinct in the park in 1914. Although environmental conditions again favor the bighorns, the vast distance between Yosemite and the nearest occupied habitat to the south made natural reoccupation in this area extremely unlikely. Thus, mountain bighorns from a southern Sierra herd were relocated to Lee Vining Canyon just east of the park, where they could become habituated to the winter range. Some of the transplanted sheep died in the first few weeks, but as spring progressed, the ewes started dropping lambs and some of the young rams began roaming into the park. The herd reached a peak of nearly 100 bighorns in 1994, but almost 60 percent of the population was killed by the winter of 1994-95. The population has rebounded since then. About 55 animals were counted in the census of 1996.

Key factors in the bighorn's extirpation here were hunting outside the park, range encroachment, and diseases introduced by domestic sheep that once grazed in the park. John Muir began his Yosemite sojourn as a sheepherder but became a vocal opponent of these "hooved locusts" for their destruction of Yosemite's high meadows. Were he alive today, he undoubtedly would rejoice at the return of the bighorn to the rocky peaks of Yosemite.

The grizzly bear, once the lord of the realm here, disappeared sometime around the 1920s. The last grizzly killed in Yosemite met its fate east of Wawona in 1895. California boasts 200 grizzly bear place names, and the bear's image adorns its flag, but the last sighting in the state occurred in Sequoia National Park in 1924. (The bruin on California's flag was sketched from a Yosemite grizzly by artist Charles Nahl.) Grizzlies, given their supreme natural power, figured prominently in Miwok mythology. No plan exists to reintroduce this archetypal North American carnivore into the park. Prime grizzly bear habitat west of the park has now been developed. Conflicts with cattle ranching would be inevitable, and the danger to people would be too great.

Fish, too, pose interesting management questions. Ice Age glaciation led to the extinction of fish over most of Yosemite's area. Fish were able to recolonize waters in the lower reaches of the Merced and Tuolumne rivers, below 4,000 feet in elevation, after the retreat of glaciers. High waterfalls formed by the glaciers, however, kept fish from repopulating higher waters. Fish are, therefore, native only to small, low-elevation areas of the park such as Yosemite Valley and below Hetch Hetchy Valley, where rainbow trout are the only native trout species.

Soon after the discovery of Yosemite by Euro-Americans, at least as early as 1877, planting of fish in higher-elevation lakes began. At first, only rainbow trout were planted, but other species, such as brook trout, brown trout, Dolly Varden, golden trout, and cutthroat trout also were introduced over the years. Systematic fish planting began shortly after the park's creation in 1892. Fish hatcheries, which are no longer in operation, were built in Wawona in 1895 and Happy Isles in 1927. Pack animals carried fingerlings during early years of fish planting, but more recently fingerlings were dropped from airplanes into Yosemite's lakes by the California Department of Fish and Game (CDFG).

Eventually, the National Park Service realized that planting of non-native fish was incompatible with the goal of preserving naturally functioning ecosystems. A program to phase out fish stocking in the park began in 1972, with stocking eventually restricted to only 13 heavily-used lakes. Fish stocking in Yosemite ceased completely in 1991.

The termination of fish stocking has been controversial. The CDFG favors stocking to provide public recreation and to generate revenues through the sale of fishing licenses, and many park visitors want to perpetuate opportunities for good catches through

pervirens, *has a more usual conifer profile and branch structure. It is named for the color of its heartwood, not its brownish bark. A third species, the dawn redwood,* Metasequoia glyptostroboides, *is indigenous to China.*

87

Ecology of the Giant Sequoia

In total volume the giant sequoia is the world's largest living thing. Boughs of mature sequoias appear to adorn stout columns rather than trunks. Single sequoia limbs may be larger than record-sized trees of many species, and there appear to be no built-in limits to these trees' growth. Sequoias do not die of old age.

From seed to sapling. Giant sequoias sprout only from seeds. Each year mature trees may produce 2,000 cones that collectively bear half a million seeds so small and light they look like oat flakes. Green, closed, and about the size of hens' eggs, cones may stay on a tree for 20 years. After four or five years lichen growth may seal them shut so they cannot release their seeds. Three agents help sequoia seeds reach the ground.
1. Fire may dry them and cause a seed explosion.

Brown cone ready to disperse seeds.

Mature
seed

Shedding
seed coat

Germinating
seed

2 weeks:
Showing four
cotyledons

2. The Douglas squirrel, or chickaree, eats the cones and releases their seeds.

3. Larvae of a tiny cone-boring beetle also help perpetuate the sequoia species. Chewing their way to the cone's inner tissue, they cut its veins. The cone then dries out and shrinks and its seeds fall to the ground. The beetle may well have been associated with the sequoia since this species' genesis 150 million years ago. The chickaree is a newcomer; squirrels evolved only 20 million years ago.

Just reaching the ground does not assure that seeds will germinate. The odds for a given seed—91,000 seeds weigh just one pound—to produce another giant like its parent are slim. A sequoia seed must fall on bare mineral soil, not pine duff, because the energy stored in the seed can produce a tap root that reaches only one inch in length. In giant sequoia groves areas of soil are generally exposed only by occasional forest fires. Fires not only bare the soil but also burn off competing smaller species such as the shade-tolerant white fir. *Fire, therefore, is vital for sequoia reproductive success.* For many years all fires were suppressed in the park, to these great trees' detriment. Since 1971 some lightning fires and prescribed burns have promoted new growth.

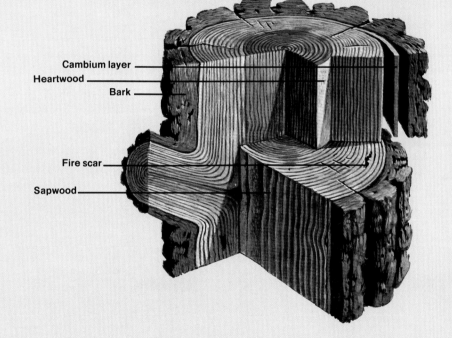

Cambium layer

Heartwood

Bark

Fire scar

Sapwood

In nature, sequoia saplings do not grow right next to the parent tree as shown here for identification purposes. White fir trees may grow this close to a sequoia, however. Their burning can leave fir scars on the sequoia's bark.

Discovering the Giant Trees

The official species discovery date for the giant sequoia is regarded as June 1852, when an article about the trees was published and circulated. The first authentic record of the giant sequoia was published in Pennsylvania in 1839, but the printing company burned to the ground before the newspapers were distributed and the article was not discovered for many years. Joseph Walker and his party were probably the first non-Indians to see the giant trees in what is now Yosemite's Tuolumne Grove in 1833, and they may also have seen the Merced Grove. The Walker party crossed the Sierra on the Indians' Mono Trail, essentially the route of the present transpark Tioga Road. The Mariposa Grove was first seen by non-Indians in 1857. The Merced Grove probably was not seen by non-Indians until 1870 during a survey for the first wagon road into Yosemite Valley.

These mammoth trees inhabited remote wilderness, and news of them met skepticism and scorn. A 20-foot cross section of a sequoia trunk shipped east in 1875 for the U.S. Centennial Exposition the next year was called a hoax. Loggers did need convincing: One giant sequoia can yield as much wood as an acre of virgin Pacific Northwest forest. To drop the largest trees required 22 days of work from four men using axes and monstrous crosscut saws.

Upon falling, the giant trunks often shattered and splintered into fragments of no economic value. Other pieces might have been too big to move and so had to be blasted into transportable chunks. Although weak and brittle, sequoia wood is phenomenally decay-resistant. It found a ready market for the manufacturing of fenceposts, shingles, and grape stakes. Large trees were also cut for exhibitions both here and abroad. A few were cut down just to *prove* how big they were. Eventually public pressure to save the 75 remaining sequoia groves, all located on the western flank of the Sierra Nevada, mounted. The movement was guided by people such as John Muir and Col. George W. Stewart, a Visalia, California, journalist. The Galen Clark tree in Yosemite's Mariposa Grove commemorates the man who explored and first publicized this grove. Clark became its first guardian after the grove and Yosemite Valley were set aside for protection in 1864. He held that position intermittently over a 30-year period.

First National Park Service Director Stephen T. Mather and his daughter pose beside a giant sequoia trunk cross section in 1928 (photo below, left). Tree-ring dating places the tree's birth at 923. The Wawona Tunnel Tree (center photo) was tunneled through as a curiosity for wagoners—and later motorists. The photo on the right shows visitors at the Mariposa Grove in 1931.

stocking. The National Park Service, therefore, must weigh ecological, sociological, and political factors when making such decisions. In this case, the National Park Service determined that ecological costs of continued fish stocking were too great, recognized that self-perpetuating fish populations would continue to provide good fishing in a large number of park lakes, and negotiated satisfactory agreements with the CDFG.

If there is an animal that symbolizes national parks, it is the black bear. You may not see one in Yosemite, but if you do, it will be an exciting experience—even from the safe distance you are advised to keep.

To the casual observer self-sustaining populations of trout in Yosemite lakes may seem perfectly natural. And black bears, having no natural enemies except humans, appear natural. Were there trout in Yosemite lakes before the Ice Age glaciers lumbered through, killed them off, and left waterfalls that isolated them? Was there a time when grizzly bears were—as now—not present to share this community with black bears?

As a baseline for its resources management program the National Park Service adopts the ideal of a pristine Yosemite. Ecological processes were largely undisturbed here when the men of the Mariposa Battalion rode their horses down into Yosemite Valley. The Ahwahneechee living in the Valley before its 1851 entry by non-Indians did not greatly disturb the ecological integrity of the areas they used. Park managers therefore take the environment of that period as the ecological benchmark for restorations and reintroductions. But even at that, no one seriously proposes to bring back the grizzly bear, because the park area alone could not provide adequate habitat. And park managers have no plans to poison those hundred and more Yosemite lakes that now contain trout but did not in 1850.

Ecologically there is much we do not know. We must simply work with nature to the best of our present understanding. Patient cooperation, listening, and astute observation increase wisdom. Pressures from within and without the park, even from other hemispheres, and the reality of many previous disruptions of the natural regime preclude our exercising unequivocally the ultimate wisdom of letting nature be.

Wildflowers

Western azalea

Whorled penstemon

Mariposa lily

Mountain violet

Cinquefoil

Orchid

Clarkia

Goldenrod and yarrow

94

California poppy

Purple nightshade

Lady-slipper orchid

Jeffery shooting star

Spicebush

Common monkeyflower

Western tanager

Great gray owl

Mountain bluebird

Acorn woodpecker

Red-winged blackbird

White-crowned sparrow

California gull

Lazuli bunting

Red-tailed hawk

Red-tailed hawk young

Great horned owl

Western bluebird

Mountain quail

Cedar waxwing

97

Mammals

Coyote

Bighorn sheep

Red fox

Mule deer

California ground squirrel

Deer mouse

Raccoon

Belding ground squirrel

Bobcat kittens

Pika

Ringtail

Mountain lion

Yellow-bellied marmot

Golden-mantled ground squirrel

Black bear

Badger

99

About 250 to 500 black bears roam Yosemite. Grizzly bears once also inhabited the park, but they were hunted to extinction in California sometime subsequent to 1920. The number of black bears found in any given area of Yosemite can vary widely with habitat type and season, but an estimated 5 to 20 forage in Yosemite Valley.

Mating is the only time adult black bear males and females associate. They mate in early to mid-summer, but the fertilized eggs do not implant in the female's uterus until late fall. Gestation is just six to eight weeks. Cubs are born in the hibernation den during mid-January to February in litters most commonly of one to three cubs. Newborn cubs are blind, naked, and weigh less than a pound. They emerge from the den with their mother in March or April weighing 8 to 10 pounds and can weigh as much as 100 pounds by late fall. The cubs will stay with their mother through the following winter and spring, a total of about a year and a half. Although they

The National Park Service now pursues a rigorous human-bear management program. Its purpose is to restore the natural distribution and behavior of bears and to prevent personal injuries and property damage that might occur in situations like that in the above photograph.

are classified as carnivores, black bears eat mostly plant material such as grasses, nuts, and berries. Most protein in their diet comes from insects such as termites, ants, and beetle grubs. As winter approaches, the bears feed heavily on high-calorie foods, such as acorns and fruits, and can enter their winter dens weighing as much as 50 percent more than they did in spring.

At one time, feeding stations and open dump sites in the park provided visitors with entertaining views of foraging black bears. The food sources, however, seriously altered the behavior, population dynamics, and ecological role of park bears. The last feeding station in Yosemite was closed in the late 1950s and the last open dump was shut in the early 1970s. Subsequently the National Park Service has spent millions of dollars to further reduce human food availability to bears by fitting all trash cans and dumpsters with bear-resistant lids and installing food storage lockers in every campsite. Human carelessness, however, is undermining these efforts. In 1996, property damage in Yosemite from bears reached nearly $350,000, and more than 90 percent of that occurred to motor vehicles. Unfortunately, this carelessness is costing the lives of bears. Several bears must be killed each year after they become dangerously aggressive in seeking human food. Current efforts are aimed at informing visitors about this problem and gaining compliance with food storage regulations.

Profile
of black bear

Backpackers must store their food properly to avoid property damage, interrupted trips, and "corruption" of bears. One accepted method is counterbalancing, whereby food is suspended high up and far out on the limbs of a tree (for instructions see literature issued with wilderness permits).

Better yet, store food in park-approved bear-resistant food canisters, which are available for purchase or rent in several park locations. The canisters are easier to use and more secure than counterbalancing.

101

The Ahwahneechee

People may have visited the Yosemite region intermittently as early as 8,000-10,000 years ago. About 4,000 years ago people had begun to settle in Yosemite Valley. About A. D. 1000 to 1200, a culture recognizable as the predecessor of the Southern Sierra Miwok was established in the region. These people were the ancestors of people who still live in Yosemite. The Southern Miwok believe themselves to have been created in the land they still call home. The Indians who lived in Yosemite Valley made up only one division of these people. They called their home Ahwahnee, meaning "valley that looks like a gaping mouth," and themselves the Ahwahneechee, meaning "dwellers in Ahwahnee." Living in Yosemite Valley during summer, many apparently migrated down to the Sierra foothills for the winter. The Ahwahneechee's contact with outsiders was principally for trade. From coastal tribes near the Pacific Ocean, the people obtained abalone and other shells they valued highly. On the east side of the Sierra Nevada lived the Mono Lake Paiute people, whose language and customs were different from the Miwok. Although regarded with suspicion by most Miwok, these people were the only source of items the Miwok wanted, such as obsidian, pine nuts, rabbit-skin blankets, and insect foods. In return, the Yosemite Miwok exchanged black bracken fern root (used for patterns in baskets), acorns, manzanita berries, and other items. Their hunting-and-gathering lifestyle centered on seeds, the protein-rich acorns of the black oak, numerous native greens, bulbs, deer, and trout. Specialized methods of gathering these foods, as well as specific cooking techniques, had been developed over the centuries the people lived here. The arrival of the Spaniards on the California coast in the late 1700s had little impact on the Sierra Miwok. The missions that the Spaniards built to convert the Indian people to Christianity declined in the early 1800s. Many of the natives left the coast to live in the Sierra foothills, bringing their exposure to Spanish food, clothing, and technology with them.

Forming villages with resident Miwok people, they raided ranchos on the coast and drove herds of horses to the Sierra, where horse flesh became a major food source. Few non-Indians ventured into the Sierra Nevada before the 1840s, but the discovery of gold in 1848 prompted a flood of miners into the foothills west of Yosemite. The miners' destruction of resources and ecosystems in their zeal to strike it rich ruined the food sources which sustained the Miwok. Conflicts between the Indians and miners were common.

Miners fought the Indians in the foothills but would lose track of them as they retreated into the mountains. The Mariposa Battalion was formed in 1851, under the authority of the governor of California, to put an end to the conflicts. The battalion, eventually following a group of Indian people into the mountains, became the first documented non-Indians to enter Yosemite Valley. Some of Yosemite's native people were relocated for a few months to the Fresno River Reservation, and the battalion was disbanded.

A Miwok/Paiute ceremony held in June 1872 at the current site of the Yosemite Lodge

Indian Village

The Indian Village behind the Valley Visitor Center interprets the Indian people of Ahwahnee in the year 1872, 20 years after their initial contact with non-Indians. The killing of two miners in Yosemite Valley in 1852 had led to the organization of a second battalion that executed five Yosemite Indians for purportedly killing the miners. In just a few years life had changed dramatically for the Ahwahneechee. By the mid-1850s local residents were befriending them, and they participated in treaty negotiations with commissioners of both federal and local governments. Most people wore clothes cast off by whites or purchased with gold they had panned from local streams. New foods such as bread and tortillas became popular. By the 1870s Paiute people from Mono Lake, with whom the Yosemite had long traded, began to settle in Yosemite Valley, apparently lured by the prospect of employment by local businesses. Hotels employed Indian people as housekeepers, laundresses, guides, and stable hands and bought trout from them to put on hotel restaurant tables. Indian people continued to live in established native villages in Yosemite Valley into the early years of this century. In the 1930s the National Park Service established a new Indian Village, moving the residents of the last village into the new houses. In the 1960s some of the people left Yosemite, older members of the tribal group died, and a few families moved into National Park Service residential areas with other employees. In 1970 the local native people formed the American Indian Council of Mariposa County to give themselves a voice in affairs that

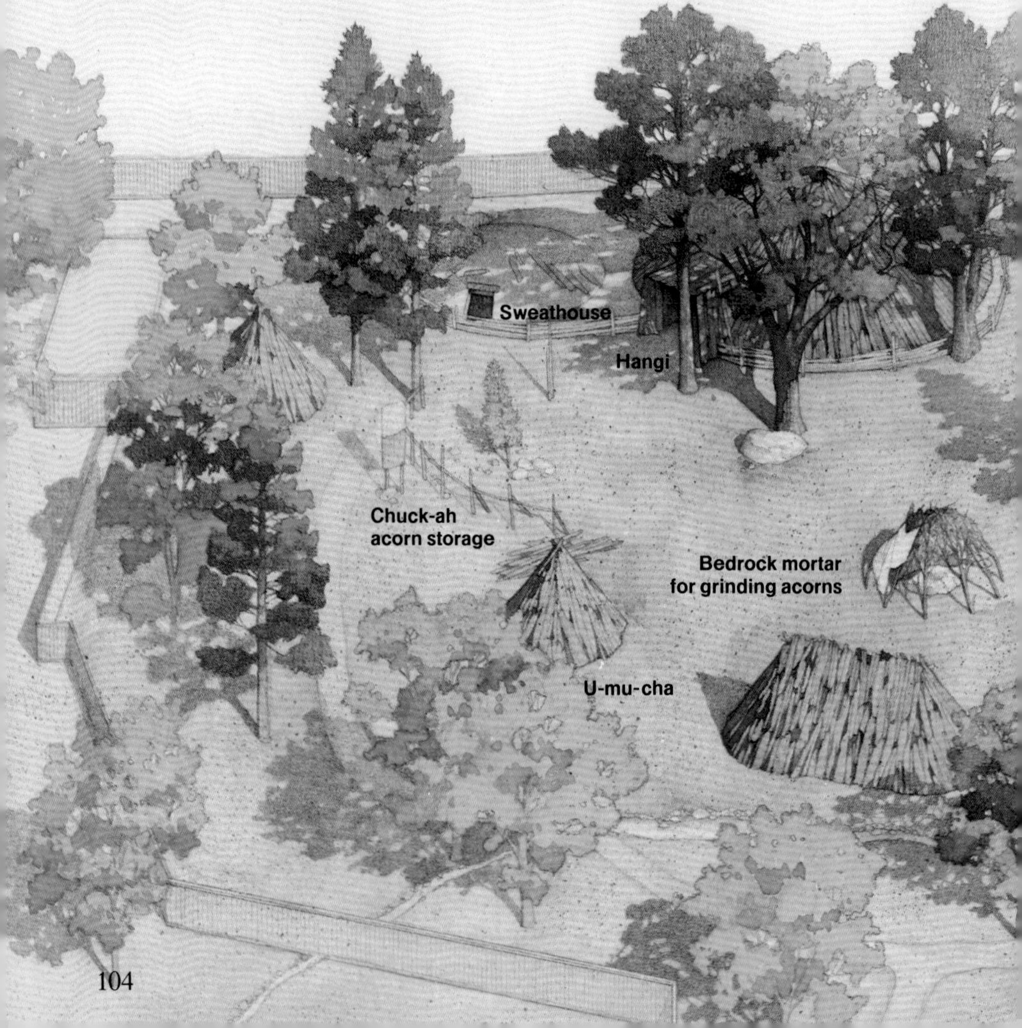

Sweathouse

Hangi

Chuck-ah acorn storage

Bedrock mortar for grinding acorns

U-mu-cha

concern them. Today a few families of native Miwok and Paiute people live in Yosemite Valley, where they are employed by the National Park Service, while other descendents live in Mariposa County and throughout the western United States.

In 1872, the staple food remained black oak acorns, collected in the fall. Acorns were stored in granaries called *chuck-ahs*. These simple structures of incense-cedar or pine poles, grapevine, and willow, deerbrush, or white fir branches were lined with wormwood to discourage insect intrusions. They were capped with pine needles, wormwood, and incense-cedar bark. Ponderosa pine boughs were used as thatching. *Chuck-ahs* could hold up to 500 pounds of acorns. Acorns were dried, shelled, pounded, and sifted and the resulting flour leached to remove its tannic acid. The leaching produced flours in three grades. The finest was used for thin soup. The mid-grade was used for mush. The coarsest flour was used to make loaves of a jelly-like consistency. The *hangi*, or roundhouse, was built of oak posts and shingled with incense-cedar bark. It served ceremonial purposes—dancing and prayer—and still does. The smaller sweathouse was used for purification before dancing or hunting. The Miwok dwelling, called *u-mu-cha*, was built of pine and cedar poles thatched with incense-cedar bark. By the 1890s this traditional dwelling was giving way to homes fashioned after simple pioneer cabins.

U-mu-cha

Leaching bed
for acorns

U-mu-cha

105

The Indian Cultural Exhibit

The Yosemite Museum adjacent to the Valley Visitor Center depicts the culture of the native people of the Yosemite region. It is not only a place where Miwok, Paiute, Chukchansi Yokuts, and Mono people of all ages can see evidence of their heritage, but also where others can learn and appreciate the cultural traditions developed by these people over the centuries. Included in the exhibits is a diorama of a late 19th century Miwok-Paiute family and their home, and a hands-on exhibit of games and utilitarian objects. Some exhibits commemorate individual Indians, now deceased, and display examples of their handiwork. Major changes which occurred in the 19th century are highlighted in displays tracing the development of baskets made for sale to non-Indians. Perhaps the finest single collection of such baskets produced in the Yosemite-Mono Lake region is held by Yosemite National Park. Foremost in the exhibition

are pieces from the collection of the late James H. Schwabacher donated to Yosemite through the generosity of his children. Displays are changed periodically to give visitors an opportunity to see a diverse selection of materials from the Yosemite Museum collection. Demonstrations of traditional native skills include a variety of activities, such as basketry, beadwork, arrowhead and string making, netting, and games.

The art of Indian basketry in Yosemite National Park encompasses varied styles and types. These baskets represent a small sample. Traditional baskets made for native uses, including food processing and storage, are at right. The largest basket and those on the left were produced as art objects, primarily for sale to non-Indians.

Paiute-Miwok
1-3 and **6-8** Lucy Telles
4-5 Leanna Tom
Paiute
 9 Cooking basket
14 Personal mush bowl basket

Miwok
10 Nancy Wilson, cooking basket
11 Gift basket
12 Sally Ann Castagnetto, acorn flour sifting tray
13 Storage basket

Amidst Such Flux,
An Island of Stability

A vast snowfield and the Clark Range dwarf cross-country skiers in Yosemite's increasingly popular winter backcountry.

"We were married here in the valley last year, and now we're returning for our anniversary," Ron Voss and Janet Olson of San Lorenzo, California, told a writer for the Conservation Foundation. "This place is never the same," Ron said of Yosemite Valley, "yet it's like coming home." John Muir said as much of the Sierran peaks rising above and beyond Yosemite's spectacular Valley: "Going to the mountains is going home. We always find that the strangest objects in these mountain wilds are in some degree familiar, and we look upon them with a vague sense of having seen them before."

What a sense of stability Yosemite evokes! Whether you seek to stabilize your pattern of living, your psyche, or your spirit, you find comfort in the feeling that Yosemite will be here forever. One generation of rock climbers may see Yosemite Valley as a temple, the next generation as a mere gymnasium, but for both it will be there. In contrast, most American cities will be rebuilt within 50 or 100 years. Families commonly move from state to state, and in a social sea of such mobility, Yosemite constitutes an island of constancy. Amidst such flux Yosemite offers a good place to define family and interpersonal relationships.

To make such claims might suggest nostalgic speculation except that so many people return to Yosemite so many times. Yosemite boasts the National Park System's highest rate of repeat visitation, a remarkable 67 percent. Two-thirds of Yosemite's visitors have been here before. Many return time and again.

"I was born in 1921 and made my first trip to Yosemite as a baby, with my parents and grandparents," Jack Phinney reminisced. "That was in 1923. They slept me on a cot. My grandmother, who was camping with us, had done a lot of baking—cookies, buns, and bread. My folks kept these goodies in a wicker suitcase under my cot. The tent had no floor.

One night a bear came into the tent undetected, pulled that suitcase out, dragged it off about 30 yards, and ate every last piece of my grandmother's baking. The bear ate three dozen cookies, some buns, and two loaves of bread. My folks got the wicker suitcase back in the morning, with the bear's claw marks in it. Of course, I don't remember the incident," Jack said. "I was just a baby. But I remember being told about it and I remember seeing the wicker suitcase. My grandparents still used it for years after that."

According to the diary Jack's father kept of the trip, the bear raided their larder on Sunday, July 8, 1923, in Camp 14, the campground now known as Lower Pines. The next night they secured their food so the bears could not steal it.

Jack recently retired from his career in vocational arts teaching and administration in Los Angeles area public schools. For part of each year now he wears a special National Park Service uniform, not the standard ranger uniform, but a khaki shirt with a different patch. Jack is a VIP—a Volunteer-in-Parks. Many people who love national parks, such as Jack, are giving their time and talents to augment reduced Park Service staffs, enabling the Service to stretch tight budgets further.

"From the time I was a baby until I was out of high school there were only maybe two years that I didn't go to Yosemite," Jack said. "Then, when I was in the Navy aboard a heavy cruiser in the Pacific theater of World War II, I missed a couple of years. But I don't think I've missed a year since then. It just didn't seem like a complete year unless I went to Yosemite."

His father, a teacher before him, had summers off, and his family would camp in the same area every year. "You would make friends who would come up to Yosemite from year to year. Some people stayed all summer back then. Maybe the family would stay up and the fathers would work during the weeks and come up on weekends. You looked forward to seeing your Yosemite friends each summer."

When the 1930s opened, Jack was nine years old and the world of Yosemite travel was far different from today. "There were lots of bears in the Valley and bear jams on the road because the bears were still being fed. Yosemite Village was located on the south side of the Valley then, near Sentinel Bridge.

The road divided around a sequoia tree that had been planted there. It wasn't a high-speed road then, and you could drive off it anywhere, into the woods or into the meadows. I remember as a child the dance hall, movie house, and barber shop in the old Yosemite Village. There was a large open dump by Camp Curry, but it didn't seem to bother people at all. We took it for granted then."

Camping is an old tradition at Yosemite. James Mason Hutchings and his 1855 tourist party, as well as subsequent early visitors, camped with saddle and pack horses. After roads reached the Valley, wagons and buggies transported many campers and their paraphernalia even though hotels had begun springing up in the Valley in 1856, the year after Hutchings' visit.

"At a time when Yellowstone could record but a scant five hundred visitors," Freeman Tilden wrote in *The National Parks*, "Yosemite Valley was already a thriving tourist resort. There is doubt that any scenic locality ever enjoyed such a quick publicity and growth. Within a year from the day when the *Mariposa Gazette* published the account of the Hutchings tourist party's expedition into the area, a camp for travelers had been built on the south fork of the Merced, and trails for saddle parties were being pushed toward the valley floor."

Entrepreneur A. Harris built the first *public* campground in Yosemite in 1878. Camping equipment in the horse-drawn vehicle era routinely included elaborate chairs and camp stools. Such style equates, perhaps, with our camping in recreational vehicles today, but campers today do not dress formally as did those late Victorians and early Edwardians. Women sported full, collared, floor-length dresses. Men's attire ran to three-piece suits, dress shirts, and neckties, compromising with the outdoors only on the hat and boots.

"Just camping at all was considered roughing it, even in the 1920s and 1930s," Jack Phinney recalled. "You didn't have to backpack." Jack also remembered what a horrendous chore it was to wash clothes by hand in camp.

When Jack's father first camped at Yosemite in the mid-teens of this century, automobiles were subject to strict regulations whose purpose was to avoid scaring horses. Later, when cars were allowed in the Valley, a ranger would check out each car's brakes

Early Tourism

In 1874, two toll roads, the Coulterville and Yosemite Turnpike and the Big Oak Flat Road, reached the Valley. The first stagecoach arrived in July. Another toll road, an extension of the Wawona route, was added in 1875. Stages remained the popular mode of travel until automobiles, having first reached the Valley in 1900, began to supplant them in earnest in 1913 when they were officially allowed to enter the park amidst controversy about their propriety in national parks. The Yosemite Valley Railroad arrived at nearby El Portal in 1907. "The short line to paradise," people called it. At its terminus near the park's boundary, tourists transferred to stagecoaches that plied the steep Merced Canyon up to the Valley. The All-Year Highway (Highway 140) was completed in 1926. In 1945 a flood, the decline of lumbering and mining activities, and ever-increasing auto and bus travel doomed the rail service. Today's travelers still follow the patterns set by the pioneers of tourism: the Mariposa Battalion and Hutchings entered along a route close to today's **South Entrance** and Wawona. Rail travelers took the stage up today's **Arch Rock Entrance** route. **Big Oak Flat Entrance** is near the junction of the Old Big Oak Flat Road, which entered Yosemite Valley several miles east of the Coulterville Road, and the present Big Oak Flat Road, completed in 1940. In 1883 the Great Sierra Wagon Road was opened. It roughly followed the Indians' Mono Trail to Tuolumne Meadows. The Joseph Walker party, apparently the first non-Indian people to see Yosemite Valley, had followed this trail 50 years earlier. The modern Tioga Road across the park was dedicated in 1961. **Tioga Pass Entrance** welcomes today's westbound travelers on this road. The inset photo shows cars at the New Village Plaza in the Valley in 1932.

Stages and wagons from the park's early transportation history are displayed at the Pioneer Yosemite History Center at Wawona.

Early Camping

Tourism in Yosemite Valley began in 1855, a year after Lt. Tredwell Moore's account of the Mariposa Battalion's exploits appeared in the *Mariposa Chronicle*. There were perhaps 42 tourists that year; now annual visitation is more than 4 million. Notable among those first visitors was James Mason Hutchings, who came on horseback with Thomas A. Ayres, an artist. Ayres gave the world its first pictures of the Valley in *Hutchings' Illustrated California Magazine* of 1856. That same year a toll path was developed into the Valley via Mariposa and the South Fork of the Merced. Yosemite articles by Hutchings between 1856 and 1860 were collected in his book, *Scenes of Wonder and Curiosity in California*. The magazine and the book established Hutchings, who settled in the Valley in 1864, as Yosemite's chief publicist, innkeeper, and guide. Yosemite changed from a regional to a national attraction in 1859 and 1860 with accounts of visits written, respectively, by New York *Tribune* editor Horace Greeley and Unitarian minister Thomas Starr King. The Reverend King, then a resident of San Francisco, had established a reputation as a travel writer while living in Boston.

His Yosemite experiences generated six travel letters to the *Boston Evening Transcript* in 1860 and 1861. Such notables as Oliver Wendell Holmes and John Greenleaf Whittier read and commented on them. Both Greeley and King reached the Valley on horses,

which, along with mules, provided transportation until 1874. Gustav Fagersteen's photo, *Camping Party at Bridalveil Fall*, taken in 1880, shows that camping was by then a high art.

before it could go in. Jack's family camped with a lean-to style tent that went over the car: "You could open the car door and be right in your tent. "The Curry Company would rent you camping gear and hammocks and mattresses."

The year the bear wiped out their baked goods was the first year the Phinneys had an assigned campground. The assignment was made at heaquarters, and when the campers got to the campground, they just picked out any vacant spot. Campgrounds had boundaries, but no sites were designated. They camped for 10 days that summer. On the Fourth of July weekend things got crowded: "Campgrounds were so packed that tent guy lines would cross. My father recorded in his journal for July 2, 1932, that 7,015 campers were registered in Yosemite's public campgrounds."

The tenets of National Park Service interpretation that we know today originated and began to evolve—right here at Yosemite—in the 1920s. In fact, the history of Yosemite as a park in many ways constitutes a microcosmic view of the evolution of national park protection, use, and enjoyment. Other parks—Yellowstone, Glacier, Grand Canyon, Mount Rainier, Rocky Mountain, Sequoia, and Zion—soon emulated Yosemite's example of outdoor and nature education. Jack Phinney's memories of naturalist outings with C.A. (Bert) Harwell probably influenced his yen to work in Yosemite.

"Bert Harwell was an expert at bird-call imitations," Jack recalled. "For me his programs were pretty spectacular. Those were the early days of park interpretation and there was nothing to compare it to. It was exciting."

Interpretation began in parks before the National Park Service was established in 1916. The few interpreters of those early days were called naturalists, trail guides, and sometimes simply teachers. John Muir was among the early and effective interpreters of parks, mainly through his influential writings in magazines and books. Muir also occasionally guided individuals or parties of tourists and scientists through Yosemite, however informally. Muir made a great contribution to the future development of park interpretation when he inspired and motivated a young man named Enos Mills to observe, write, and speak out about parks and wilderness. Mills became an early teacher of aspiring park interpreters and one who first developed goals and principles for the practice of interpretation.

Interpretation embraces a broad mix of ranger-led activities such as walks and hikes, guided tours, campfire programs, slide talks, demonstrations, living history, creative arts, and children's activities, as well as visitor center operations and, at Yosemite, the Indian Cultural Exhibit and programs. Nonprofit cooperating associations, concessioners, and other private organzations often augment the National Park Service's program of interpretive services. In the late teens of this century Sacramento philanthropist Charles M. Goethe encountered the nature-guide movement while traveling in Europe. Goethe liked it so much that he imported the idea to the United States. Beginning in 1920, the groundwork for interpretive services in national parks was laid in Yosemite by Harold C. Bryant and Loye Holmes Miller, professors of natural sciences. The position of park naturalist was created in Yosemite in 1921, with Ansel F. Hall fulfilling its duties for two years. Bert Harwell held the post from 1929 to 1940, right through Jack Phinney's childhood and teen years.

Park museums also originated at Yosemite. Museums were not new, but no one had grasped their potential for helping people understand and enjoy national parks. With naturalist programs and museums the realization of the parks' educational possibilities took shape.

Credit for the museum idea goes to Ansel Hall. Park visitor centers, so important nationwide today, have their genesis in this concept. Historian Carl P. Russell wrote that Hall ". . . conceived the idea of establishing a Yosemite museum to serve as a public contact center and general headquarters for the interpretive program." Chris Jorgenson's former artist's studio became the first, temporary museum in 1921. Museums opened that same year in Yellowstone and Mesa Verde national parks. In 1926 the Yosemite Museum, the first permanent museum in the National Park System, was completed, soon followed by similar facilities at Yellowstone and Grand Canyon.

Jack Phinney recalled fondly the Yosemite Museum of his childhood: "I was fascinated by the

When Lady Astor refused to spend the night in Yosemite because the hotels there were too primitive, Stephen T. Mather, first director of the National Park Service, was upset. The Ahwahnee Hotel resulted from Mather's injured pride. Completed in 1927, these world-class lodgings continue to live up to the promise of the press release Mather issued for the opening: "The Ahwahnee is designed quite frankly for people who know the delights of luxurious living, and to whom the artistic and material comforts of their environment are important." To the credit of Mather and the Ahwahnee, over the years the hotel has hosted innumerable international notables, including many heads of state, from presidents to kings, princes, and princesses. To realize such a hotel in a national park, in 1925 Mather forced a merger of the park's two largest concessioners. One major result of the new company's contract was The Ahwahnee. Budgeted at $600,000, the Ahwahnee opened at a cost of $1.25 million even though it came out less elaborate than originally planned. The cost of interior decoration alone was more than a quarter million dollars. The dining hall is 130 feet long, has a three-story natural wood-beam ceiling, and can seat more than 400 diners at a time. Off the Great Lounge (shown below), a spacious refuge for guests, a solarium provides an all-weather haven. Not all guests of the Ahwahnee have arrived accustomed to its luxurious approach to living. During World War II, the Ahwahnee hosted U.S. Navy men for a three-year period in its temporary role as a convalescent hospital for rehabilitation of the sick and injured.

Imagine the Great Lounge as a dormitory for 350 sailors. Some felt their isolation in this huge walled-in Valley beneath great mountains. In 1997, a two-year $1.5 million makeover was completed at The Ahwahnee; all 123 guest rooms, parlors, gift shops, and public areas were refurbished. Today the Ahwahnee Hotel maintains its graceful elegance — just one of the many delightful surprises tucked away in Yosemite Valley.

Rock Climbing

Hanging bivouac, El Capitan

High-elevation tea

Some cracks are horizontal

Don't look down, okay?

Others are vertical

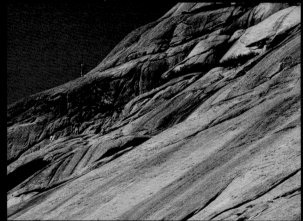

It looked small down there

Eichorn's Pinnacle...

On Glacier Point

...on Cathedral Peak

El Capitan again

Go climb a rock

Hardware for a big wall climb

Regularly scheduled programs and activities sponsored by the National Park Service and others will introduce you to the park and its resources — and to new ways to enjoy them. Interpretive programs include bird walks, bear talks, photography workshops, films, children's activities, and campfire programs.

insect specimen collections, maps, dioramas, and the live specimens. Upstairs were large cross-sections and cuts from Yosemite's big trees."

Russell maintained that ". . . the pioneer interpretive work done in Yosemite projected its influence and its personnel into the wider fields of 'nature guiding' and museum programs throughout the National Park Service." He judged the work done by Yosemite's staff as ". . . instrumental in advancing the naturalist programs in state parks and elsewhere where out-of-door nature teaching is offered to the public."

Today the National Park System probably accounts for only 10 percent of all park interpretive activities nationwide, and parks in other nations have adopted programs similar to those developed in the United States. National parks, a stable and integral component of our nation's identity, were all but born in Yosemite, and here our concept of them matured and came of age. As Jack Phinney will tell you, this ranks as one of our chief contributions to world culture. So much — and so far — has Yosemite's influence spread.

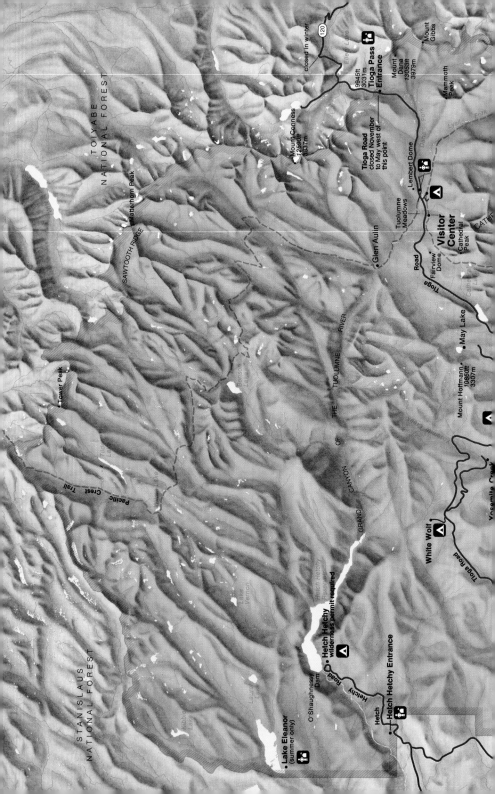

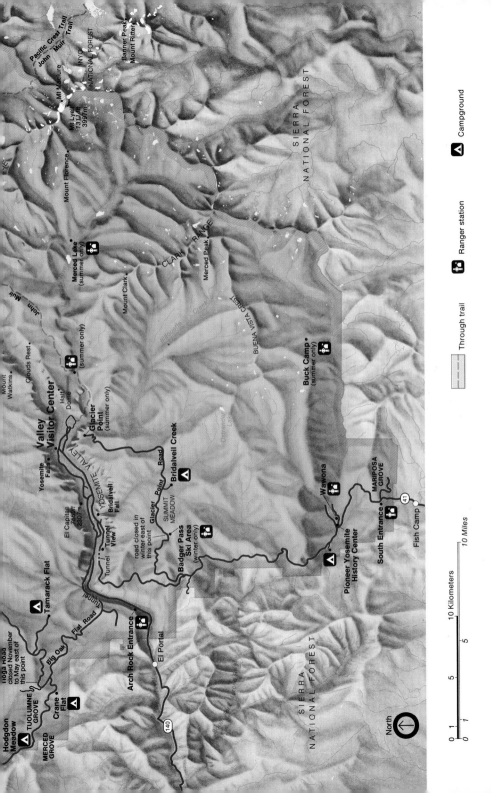

North

| 0 | 1 | 5 | 10 Kilometers |
| 0 | 1 | 5 | 10 Miles |

Through trail   Ranger station   Campground

Part 3

Guide and Adviser

**Note: Much of the information
in this section is subject to
change. Check with the park
staff before you make firm plans
based on this information.**

Vehicle Reservations   Yosemite National Park hosts more than 4 million visitors each year. Congestion has been growing since the park's 1980 General Management Plan called for measures to reduce traffic, particularly in Yosemite Valley. By 2000, the park expects to implement a reservation system for vehicles entering the park. Visitors without reservations for their car will be able to enter the park via commercial buses or shuttle buses from neighboring communities. Visitors with reservations for lodging or campsites in the park will not need a vehicle reservation to drive into the park.

About the same time, the park will be implementing plans to further reduce congestion in Yosemite Valley by requiring that visitors park their cars at designated parking areas and transfer to shuttle buses to travel around the Valley. Up-to-date information will be available as these changes occur.

By Car   Astride the Sierra Nevada crest, Yosemite lies close to the California-Nevada border. The range's steep eastern escarpment limits auto access from the east: only Route 120 East at Tioga Pass penetrates the park. Winter persists in the highcountry, and the Tioga Road may remain closed by snow as late as mid-June. Normally it is free of snow and open Memorial Day weekend to early November.

The South, Arch Rock, and Big Oak Flat entrances afford auto access to the park via the more gently inclined Sierran west slope. Route 41 connects Fresno with the South Entrance near the Mariposa Grove of Giant Sequoias. Route 140 connects Merced, Mariposa, and El Portal with the Arch Rock Entrance. Route 120 West connects Manteca with the Big Oak Flat En-

trance. You can reach Hetch Hetchy Reservoir from Route 120 about one mile northwest of the Big Oak Flat Entrance. The last miles of road are narrow (vehicles more than 25 feet in length are prohibited) and parking is limited at O'Shaughnessy Dam.

For recorded 24-hour road and weather information about Yosemite National Park, call 209-372-0200.

By Air   Fresno's airport and car rentals serve those entering the park via the South Entrance. Allow two-and-one-half hours of driving time from Fresno. Scheduled airlines intermittently serve Merced from Los Angeles and San Francisco. Driving time from Merced to the Arch Rock Entrance is less than two hours. Allow a minimum of four hours for driving from the San Francisco Bay Area airports. For daily bus service from Merced, see below.

By Rail   AMTRAK provides train service from Oakland to Merced and from Los Angeles to Fresno and Merced. For detailed information and reservations call toll-free 800-872-7245. For bus service from Fresno and Merced to Yosemite Valley, see below.

By Bus   Scheduled commercial bus lines serve Fresno and Merced from Los Angeles and San Francisco. Regularly scheduled bus service to Yosemite Valley is available from the Merced AMTRAK Station and the Transpo Center. From Fresno there is service from the AMTRAK Station and the Fresno/Yosemite Air Terminal. You can obtain current bus schedule information by calling VIA Bus Line at 800-369-7275 or 209-384-1315. Yosemite Transportation Services (YTS) connects Yosemite Valley with Tuolumne Meadows daily during the summer. Call 209-372-8441 for current YTS schedule.

Free Shuttle Bus Service Make use of the free shuttle bus service in the eastern end of Yosemite Valley. If you are visiting for the day only, park your car in the day-use parking area at Curry Village. If you are staying overnight, keep your car parked at your campground or accommodation. Limiting use of your car in the Valley reduces traffic, congestion, and pollution.

There is free shuttle bus service in the Tuolumne Meadows area from about July 1 through Labor Day. Various routes service the Tuolumne Meadows Lodge, Store, Campground, Pothole Dome, Tenaya Lake, May Lake, Tioga Pass, and some Tioga Road trailheads.

Bicycling Exercise and sightseeing mix well through bicycling in relatively level Yosemite Valley. Some eight miles of the Valley bikeway now safely separate bike traffic from automobiles. Rent single-speed bicycles by the hour or day from the Yosemite Lodge Bike Stand (year-round, weather permitting) or the Curry Village Bike Stand (summer only); fee and deposit are required. Helmets are available and are required for all riders under 18 years of age. Bicycle trailers for small children, "Baby Jogger" strollers, day packs, and wheelchair rentals are also available.

For a nice four-mile loop ride, follow the shuttle bus route from Curry Village to Happy Isles, then on to the junction at the base of the Mirror Lake hill, and return to Curry Village via the bikeway by the Upper River Campground.

Bicycles must stay on public roads, parking areas, and designated bikeway. Riding and walking bikes on foot trails or through meadows are prohibited. Ride your bicycle to ensure protection of pedestrians, other cyclists, and wildlife. On the bikeway keep to the right of the center line except to pass.

Bus Tours Yosemite Tours, based in Yosemite Valley, offers excursions through the Valley and to the Mariposa Grove of Giant Sequoias and scenic Glacier Point. Tours depart from the Ahwahnee Hotel, Curry Village, and Yosemite Lodge, and, from late spring to early autumn, in Yosemite Village. Reservations can be made at the Transportation Desks at Valley lodging facilities, and, from late spring to early autumn, at the Tour Kiosk in Yosemite Village. **Valley Floor Tour.** Operating all year, this two-hour narrated tour gives you glimpses of Half Dome, El Capitan, Bridalveil Fall, and other picturesque Valley attractions. **Mariposa Grove Tour.** Ride into the grove to see giant sequoias more than 2,500 years old. This daily six-hour tour stops for lunch at the Wawona Hotel when the hotel is open (usually mid-April until late October). **Glacier Point Tour.** Thirty miles from Yosemite Valley via road, Glacier Point provides a 270-degree panorama of Sierran peaks and an astounding view of the Valley floor 3,214 feet below. The full tour, scheduled daily during summer and fall until the road is closed by snow, lasts four hours. A special one-way rate accommodates hikers to or from Glacier Point. **Grand Tour.** This full-day outing combines the Big Trees and Glacier Point tours and is available when the Glacier Point road is open. **Tuolumne Meadows Hikers Bus.** This all-day excursion includes stops at Olmsted Point and Tenaya Lake View. Popular with day hikers and backpackers alike, this bus departs the Valley each morning (July 1 to Labor Day, conditions permitting), with stops at Crane Flat and White Wolf on the way to and from Tuolumne Meadows Lodge. Hikers can arrange to get off at trailheads and be picked up on return.

Useful Addresses and Telephone Numbers *Phone numbers are area code 209 unless listed otherwise.*

National Park Service, P.O. Box 577, Yosemite National Park, CA 95389. Park business office, phone 372-0200. **For general park information call 372-0265, or access the park's Web site at http://www.nps.gov/yose.**

Yosemite Association, P.O. Box 230, El Portal, CA 95318, 379-2648. Call this number for information about books, trail maps, and art prints available from this nonprofit membership organization that supports the park's interpretive, educational, and scientific programs. For general park information, call 900-454-9673. YA also sponsors the Yosemite Field Seminars, the Yosemite Theater, and a variety of other special activities that augment the National Park Service's interpretive program. Catalogs and brochures are available on request.

Yosemite Concession Services Corporation, 5410 East Home Avenue, Fresno, CA 93727, 252-4848. Call this number to obtain reservations for accommodations and information about other concessioner services, including Badger Pass winter sports, offered in the park.

Make camping reservations by calling, toll free, 800-436-PARK 7 a.m. to 7 p.m. Pacific time. See page 133.

For recorded information on weather and road conditions call 372-0200; lost-and-found items 379-1001; medical appointments 372-4637; and dental services 372-4200.

Deaf persons with their own TTY may get park information by calling 372-4726, room reservations at 255-8345, and camping reservations at, toll free, 888-530-9797.

In case of an emergency call 911.

Yosemite Guide Current activities, facilities, services, and safety tips are listed in the park's free newspaper, the *Yosemite Guide.* Pick up a copy at any entrance or ranger station, visitor center, or other public facility.

Outside-the-Park Lodging, Activities
Yosemite Area Traveller Information (YATI)
369 W. 18th Street
Merced, CA 95340
900-454-YOSE
http://www.yosemite.com

Tuolumne County Visitors Bureau
P.O. Box 4020
55 West Stockton Street
Sonora, CA 95370
533-4420 or 800-446-1333

Yosemite Sierra Visitor Bureau
P.O. Box 1998
41729 Highway 41
Oakhurst, CA 93644
683-4636

Coulterville Visitor Center
P.O. Box 333
5007 Main Street
Coulterville, CA 95311
878-3074

Mariposa Visitor Center
P.O. Box 425
5158 Highway 140
Mariposa, CA 95338
966-2456 or 888-555-7081

Lee Vining Chamber of Commerce and Mono Lake Visitor Center
P.O. Box 130
Highway 395 and 3rd Street
Lee Vining, CA 93541
760-647-6629 or 647-6595

Make optimum use of your time in the park by stopping at a visitor center as soon as you can. Visitor centers offer information on weather, road and trail conditions, and the availability of campsites. Audiovisual programs and exhibits describe features and other things you can see and do in the time you have available. Rangers at the information desks can answer your questions and advise you on activities and features of interest. Books and maps sold at these outlets are useful planning tools and can add to your enjoyment after your trip, too. These publications are sold by the nonprofit Yosemite Association as a benefit both to visitors and to the National Park Service.

Valley Visitor Center   Located in Yosemite Village, the Valley Visitor Center presents exhibits and information resources you should not miss. A video program describes for visitors who have just one day in the park the best way to see Yosemite. Relief models provide bird's-eye views of the Valley and the entire park. An orientation program shown throughout each day offers a guide to the park. Still other exhibits illustrate and explain geological formations and processes, describe how Yosemite came to be a national park, and interpret plant and wildlife relationships, including bears. Ask about scheduled programs in the visitor center auditoriums.

Yosemite Museum   What was life like for the Miwok people who lived in Yosemite Valley before the gold rush drew non-Indian people to this region? Many answers are found in the **Indian Cultural Exhibit** adjacent to the Valley Visitor Center. Here are displayed baskets, tools, and other artifacts of Miwok culture. During the summer Indian Cultural Interpreters demonstrate basketry, food preparation, and other arts and crafts in a model Indian Village that has been recreated behind the museum and visitor center. See pages 102-107. The **Museum Gallery** adjacent to the Indian Cultural Exhibit features changing thematic displays of historic and contemporary paintings, photographs, and other works of art. The pieces exhibited capture the dramatic landscapes, subtle intricacies, and countless moods of Yosemite, each reflecting the artist's personal response to the moment.

Wilderness Center   Located in Yosemite Village between the Ansel Adams Gallery and the post office, the Wilderness Center has displays and information on pre-trip wilderness planning, minimum impact camping techniques, and Yosemite wilderness issues. Wilderness permits are available.

Nature Center at Happy Isles   Reached by free shuttle bus at the upper end of the Valley, the Nature Center at Happy Isles offers exhibits and nature programs during the summer and early fall. Check the *Yosemite Guide* for programs and schedules.

LeConte Memorial Lodge   Located in Yosemite Valley near Housekeeping Camp, the LeConte Memorial Lodge, Yosemite's first public visitor center, houses a library, exhibits, and an environmental education program. Operated by the Sierra Club, it is open seasonally.

Mariposa Grove Museum   Open from about mid-May to mid-October, when trams are operating in the grove, this rustic log structure houses exhibits that interpret the natural history of the giant sequoias.

Pioneer Yosemite History Center
Furnished historic buildings, most of them relocated from their original settings elsewhere in the park, and horse-drawn wagons are displayed at the Pioneer Yosemite History Center at Wawona. In summer, stage rides carry passengers across the wooden covered bridge, still on its original site, sparking to life this vignette of Yosemite's pioneer past. Interpreters in period dress offer living history during the summer by portraying people and activities that helped shape Yosemite's history and its destiny as a national park. Nearby, the Wawona Hotel, still operating, provides a beautiful glimpse of an earlier tourist era. Historic Hill's Studio, on the hotel grounds, is open on a limited schedule in summer displaying reproductions of artworks from the park's museum collection.

Tuolumne Meadows Visitor Center
Usually open from Memorial Day weekend through September, Tuolumne Meadows Visitor Center provides full information services and publications. Exhibits offer John Muir's perspective on the meaning and values of Yosemite with quotations from the early naturalist and conservation writer. Exhibits feature geology, wildflowers, alpine and subalpine ecology, bears, wildlife, and the area's human history.

Parsons Lodge Located near Soda Springs at Tuolumne Meadows, this historic structure, built by the Sierra Club in 1915, is now operated intermittently during summer as an information and interpretive facility. Exhibits focus on the human history of the Tuolumne Meadows area. Parsons Lodge is a one-mile walk from the Lembert Dome parking area.

Children's walks, sunset talks at Glacier Point, night prowls of Sierran meadows, and a variety of other ranger-conducted activities offer memorable park experiences. Schedules appear in the *Yosemite Guide.* Varying in length and duration, events are listed by location, type of subject or activity, and time. Activities at or near visitor centers also are posted on bulletin boards at the centers and in campgrounds.

Programs offer delightful insights into Yosemite's wonders, past and present, and include bird walks, bear talks, geology hikes, campfire programs, films, and a myriad of other offerings that will better acquaint you with the park's resources and values. Yosemite Theater (admission fees) presents programs of live stage theater and music, and free instruction in various creative arts is offered at the **Art Activity Center** in Yosemite Valley.

The Yosemite Concession Services Corporation and the Ansel Adams Gallery, park concessioners, also offer evening programs and photography walks, seminars, and workshops. During the summer an Eastman Kodak Company photo specialist leads camera walks and presents slide programs on photography. Check the *Yosemite Guide.*

Wayside Exhibits, Roadside Markers
Outdoor exhibits along park roads, at trailheads, and in campgrounds and parking areas interpret natural and historical features and warn of safety hazards. Markers along major park roads are keyed to descriptions in the *Yosemite Road Guide,* which is sold throughout the park.

Yosemite offers overnight accommodations ranging from public campgrounds to the Yosemite Concession Services Corporation's tent cabins, housekeeping camp units, cabins, lodges, and hotels. Food services range from convenience store to market shopping, and from fast food to cafeteria fare and restaurants. Reservations are required for some lodgings and restaurants; they are advised wherever available, particularly in summer.

Information and reservations for all **overnight lodging,** including tent cabins, housekeeping camp units, and the High Sierra Camps, can be obtained from the Yosemite Concession Services Corporation, 5410 East Home Avenue, Fresno, CA 93727. You can do this in person 8 a.m. to 5 p.m. Monday through Friday, by writing, or by telephoning 252-4848.

What **meal services** are available? **Yosemite Lodge:** Yosemite Lodge Cafeteria; Garden Terrace Restaurant (no lunches); and Mountain Room Restaurant (dinner only). **Ahwahnee Hotel:** Dining room, reservations and semiformal dress required for dinner. **Wawona Hotel:** Dining room, buffet luncheon, usually April through October. **Curry Village:** Dining Pavilion serves breakfast and dinner cafeteria-style, usually April through October; hamburger stand serves fast foods, usually April through October. **Yosemite Village:** Degnan's Pasta Place serves lunch and dinner, usually May through October; hamburger stand serves fast foods, usually April through October.

For lodging and camping information outside the park, see page 130 and check the *Yosemite Guide* and visitor centers for listings of community Chambers of Commerce and local Forest Service telephone numbers, or call 900-454-YOSE.

Camping   Reservations are required in Yosemite Valley's auto campgrounds year-round. Summer through fall, reservations are also required for Hodgdon Meadow, Crane Flat, Wawona, and 50 percent of the sites at Tuolumne Meadows. Campground reservations can be made up to three months in advance by calling, toll free, 800-436-PARK, or 301-722-1257 for international callers, or by writing National Park Reservation System (NPRS), P.O. Box 1600, Cumberland, MD 21502. All other campgrounds are first-come, first-served. Telephone 372-0200 for recorded campground information.

First-come, first-served campgrounds are generally full by noon during the summer. A maximum of six persons, including children, is allowed per campsite. Fees are charged at all park campgrounds. Check for limits on how long you can stay. **Camping is permitted only in designated campgrounds.** Register at your campground by following instructions posted at its entrance. All campgrounds have restrooms or toilets. No utility hookups are available in the park. Dump stations are available in Yosemite Valley year-round and at Wawona and Tuolumne Meadows during summer. Check at visitor centers or look for information at your campground about wood collecting and fire restrictions. Firewood collection is prohibited in the Valley and above 9,600 feet. Cutting standing trees or attached limbs, alive or dead, is prohibited, as is the use of chainsaws.

All Campers Please Note: Yosemite is bear habitat. Federal law requires that all food be properly stored at all times. All campgrounds have food-storage lockers and bear-proof garbage dumpsters. Use them.

Samplings of Yosemite's hiking options fill books: short walks to scenic waterfalls or among giant trees, arduous hikes to breathtaking vistas, multi-day rambles among mountain heights. To pick a walk tailored to your interests and physical condition, get the advice of a ranger at a visitor center, information station, or permit outlets. "Hiking from Yosemite Valley," a free brochure available at the Valley Visitor Center, describes nine hikes and the distance, hiking time, and difficulty of each. Trails in Yosemite's highcountry may still be closed by snow when all traces of winter have long since left the Valley. Check on trail conditions at visitor centers or at wilderness permit outlets. All hikers—not just backcountry overnight campers—should read and heed the information about bears and drinking water on page 135. **Please remember:** All overnight wilderness use requires a permit—see Wilderness Permits, next page.

John Muir Trail Stretching between Yosemite on the north and Whitney Portal on the south, the John Muir Trail extends 211 miles through the heart of the Sierra. Most of the trail lies above 7,000 feet in elevation, some of it above 14,000 feet. For 37 miles the trail crosses the park, with road contact in Yosemite Valley and at Tuolumne Meadows. Best trail travel times are between July 15 and September 15. Pack stock sometimes cannot negotiate snow-clad high passes even in August. Wilderness permits are required for overnight stays in the park and in national forests (see Wilderness Permits). Possession and use of firearms are prohibited in national parks. National forests discourage firearms, except during hunting season. *Starr's Guide to the High Sierra Region* provides John Muir Trail information and a map. For trip planning information write to Wilderness Permits at the park address.

High Sierra Camps Loop A moderate 50.4-mile route, this loop links five High Sierra Camps and Tuolumne Meadows Lodge. In most years these camps are in operation by early July and stay open through Labor Day weekend. With their food service and tent-cabin accommodations you can trek the High Sierra with a day pack or travel on horseback unencumbered with gear. So popular is this route, however, that the National Park Service has set a quota on the number of hikers using it. Backcountry reservations must be made well in advance here. Due to high demand, reservations for the High Sierra Camps are booked by lottery. Applications are accepted from October 15 to November 30 only. The lottery is held in mid-December, and lottery applicants are notified at the end of March as to their standing in the lottery. Lottery applications are accepted in writing only. For an application contact the High Sierra Desk, Yosemite Reservations, 5410 E. Home Avenue, Fresno, CA 93727.

Hiking Sense and Safety Non-skid hiking shoes or boots will serve you best. Tennis shoes and heavy socks may suffice on some trails, but sturdier footgear is recommended. Please stay on trails. Taking shortcuts is dangerous and causes damaging erosion. Dogs and other pets are prohibited on all trails except paved paths on the floor of Yosemite Valley. Pets must be on a leash at all times. Bicycles, motorcycles, and motor vehicles are prohibited on trails. **Smoking while traveling on trails is prohibited;** you may smoke while stopped. Do not drink untreated water or contaminate lakes and streams. Dispose of human waste properly. Please carry out all trash. Horses and mules have the right-of-way on all trails. As stock approaches you, step to the uphill side of the trail, if possible, and remain quiet while the animals pass.

Wilderness Permits   All overnight backcountry use requires a wilderness permit unless you are staying at a High Sierra Camp. The permit system helps assure each party a wilderness experience and can serve as an aid during search-and-rescue operations. Information from the permit system also helps the National Park Service protect Yosemite's popular wilderness and mitigate impacts on its fragile resources by regulating use.

In the park you can get wilderness permits at the Wilderness Center in Yosemite Valley, Tuolumne Meadows Permit Kiosk (seasonal), Wawona Ranger Station, and the Big Oak Flat Information Station. Call 372-0200 for locations of open permit stations and their hours. Reservations for wilderness permits are available from 24 weeks to two days in advance of the trip start date. They can be made by writing to Wilderness Permits, P.O. Box 545, Yosemite, CA 95389, or by calling 372-0740. There is a $3 per person fee for all reservation requests. Up to 50 percent of each trailhead's daily capacity may be reserved; the rest is filled on a first-come, first-served basis the day of or one day in advance of your trip.

For hikes out of Tuolumne Meadows, to Little Yosemite Valley, or to Half Dome, you are encouraged to **make a reservation** or to **pick up your permit a day ahead.** Daily trailhead quotas in these popular areas are frequently filled. Include alternate trailheads or dates when applying for popular trailheads, particularly with Friday or Saturday departures.

Trip Planning   General information about backpacking in Yosemite is supplied with your wilderness permit. **Read this material carefully** for your safety and to avoid disappointments with logistics. Your reservation request must include: 1. Starting and ending dates; 2. Trailhead(s); 3. Destination; and 4. Number of people and stock animals. Keep your party size small. Smaller groups are easier to accommodate on already heavily booked trailheads. Maximum group size is 15, or eight for any cross-country or off-trail hiking. Stock is limited to 25 head and is permitted only on established trails. Write or call the Yosemite Association for its mail-order literature list. Maps and books will enhance both your pre-trip planning and your ultimate appreciation of Yosemite.

Bear Warning   Some 250 to 500 bears inhabit the park area. Your wilderness permit packet includes instructions on storing your food to prevent bears from getting at it. The National Park Service recommends purchasing or renting bear-resistant food canisters for reliable backcountry food storage. These are available at several outlets throughout the park. Violations of federal law requiring proper food storage in bear habitat carry fines of up to $5,000. The National Park Service is committed to breaking the link between Yosemite's bears and human food sources and enforces the law.

Water Warning   *Giardia lamblia,* a protozoan, may contaminate any surface water, no matter how clean it looks. Drink only water from approved public supplies or water that has been boiled for three to five minutes. Iodine or a "*Giardia*-rated" filter is also an effective method of treatment. Feces of humans and some domestic and wild animals carry *Giardia.* To help prevent transmission of this disease, bury your waste at least four to six inches deep and at least 100 feet from any water or watercourse.

Hypothermia Dangers See Winter Activities for important information on this all-season killer. Hypothermia can occur even when air temperatures are as high as 50°F.

Trailhead Parking Thefts from cars parked overnight at trailheads sometimes occur. Lock your car thoroughly and do not leave valuables visible. It is best to lock valuables in a car trunk. To discourage bears from damaging your vehicle, do not leave any food in vehicles at trailheads. Store ice chests and other items that may resemble food packaging out of sight.

Horse Use Recreational use of horses, mules, burros, and llamas is appropriate in Yosemite. Wilderness regulations and other provisions listed above apply. Please contact the park to get a copy of "Information for Stock Users in Yosemite National Park" **before your visit.** It offers travel and safety tips and information on head limits, travel restrictions, trail closures, grazing, unloading, and overnight boarding of stock, and bear and other safety warnings. Stock and riders with limited mountain experience may have trouble since much of Yosemite's backcountry is above 8,000 feet in elevation. Arrange guided trail rides with Yosemite Concession Services Corporation liveries by telephoning 372-8348.

Much of Yosemite's spectacular dome and big-wall scenery is composed of high-quality granite. With its generally good summer and fall weather and ease of access, the park—particularly Yosemite Valley—has become an international mecca for rock climbing. Few climbers can long resist its challenge of near-vertical walls. Many advanced climbing techniques and even tools have been developed here. The park's most popular climbing areas are Yosemite Valley, Tuolumne Meadows, and sites along the Tioga Road. The climbing season usually extends from April into October.

Yosemite Valley The Valley offers many grade I through VI climbs. El Capitan alone boasts more than 75 grade VI routes. Shorter routes abound in the 5.7 to 5.11 Yosemite Decimal System category. There are some 5.12 and 5.13 routes. Yosemite is famous for its long, difficult crack climbs. Weather can be a double threat in summer. Hot days can bring dehydration, heat exhaustion, and heat stroke. Temperatures can drop below freezing in June, and rains can be cold in any month. The danger is hypothermia, the rapid and potentially fatal lowering of body temperature.

Tuolumne Meadows Tuolumne has grade I to IV routes that vary from 5.6 to 5.12 in difficulty. Most climbs are on glacially polished granite domes. Tuolumne is located on the Tioga Road (see map) and can be reached by car from about Memorial Day through early November. The elevation is 8,600 feet, and winter snows lie from three to nine feet deep. Many climbers prefer Tuolumne to the Valley in summer because it is cooler and less crowded.

Summer weather is generally excellent for climbing, but snow, hail, and rainstorms can occur in any month. Occasional afternoon thunderstorms can be severe.

Wilderness Areas Yosemite's wilderness is accessible on foot from about June 1 through October. It offers many fine rock climbs on peaks in the 13,000-foot range, but be wary of the weather. It can go from sunny to a snow squall within minutes. The granite is fractured with much loose rock; most climbers wear helmets, a prudent precaution. Low-angle ice and snow climbing (25 to 40°) can be pursued on several small glaciers. Backcountry rock climbs feature grade I to IV routes that vary from 5.0 to 5.13 in difficulty.

Climbers note: Free wilderness permits are required for **all multi-day wilderness trips.**

Climbing Books, Route Maps Books and maps are available at visitor centers, in the mountain shops at Tuolumne Meadows and Curry Village, and by mail from the Yosemite Association. The several books that detail park routes include *Yosemite Climbs: Free Climbs* and *Yosemite Climbs: Big Walls,* both by Don Reid, and *Rock Climbs of Tuolumne Meadows* by Don Reid and Chris Falkenstein.

Safety Rock climbing and scrambling are leading causes of injury and death in the park. **Remember:** If you are inexperienced, it is difficult to assess the hazards of a route from below. A fall of less than six feet can cause serious injury or even death. Get proper training and equipment before you climb or scramble and take enough time to work safely.

Climbing Instruction Rock climbing is taught in the park by the staff of the Yosemite Mountaineering School, Yosemite National Park, CA 95389. Write for rates and information.

Safety Rock climbing and scrambling are leading causes of injury and death in the park. **Remember:** If you are inexperienced, it is difficult to assess the hazards of a route from below. A fall of less than six feet can cause serious injury or even death. Get proper training and equipment before you climb or scramble—and take enough time to work safely. Registration for climbs is voluntary but encouraged; register at the visitor center or ranger station nearest the area of your planned climb.

Boating and Floating   Rafting as a recreational activity is being increasingly regulated to protect fragile river and river-side resources. At some point in the near future, rafting may be discontinued on the Merced River in Yosemite Valley.

Yosemite Valley   Kayaks, canoes, and rafts may be used on the Merced River in the Valley without a permit. From Stoneman Bridge to Sentinel Beach swimming aids such as life preservers, inner tubes, and air mattresses may be used. A U.S.C.G.-approved personal flotation device is required for each floater under conditions of heavy runoff (usually from spring until mid-summer). **The Merced is closed to all swimmers, rafters, and boaters when water conditions are too hazardous for safe use.** Check with a ranger or at a visitor center for up-to-date information.

Boating on Lakes   Boats and other craft without motors may be used on the following lakes: Tenaya, Merced, May, Benson, Tilden, Twin, Kibbie, and Many Islands. Special permits for boating on any other park lakes must be obtained from the Superintendent. Permits are seldom granted except for necessary park operations. Boating is not permitted on Hetch Hetchy Reservoir. All craft on the lakes listed above must carry a U.S.C.G.-approved personal flotation device for each person aboard.

Horseback Riding   The availability of horseback riding in Yosemite is subject to change. Riding stables at Wawona, Tuolumne Meadows, and Yosemite Valley rent mounts for guided trail rides. The Valley Stables operate from Easter to mid-October, the others in summer only. Reservations are advised for all rides. Two-hour Valley rides go to Mirror Lake. During summer, half-day rides lead from the Valley to the top of Nevada Fall, and an all-day ride goes to Glacier Point for stunning vistas of Half Dome, Vernal and Nevada falls, and Sierran peaks sprawling to the horizon.

Hang Gliding   Hang gliding from Glacier Point is permitted only for those with a Hang IV certification and only through the sponsorship of the Yosemite Hang Gliding Association. For reservations call 719-632-8300.

Five species of trout inhabit park waters: rainbow, brook, brown, golden, and cutthroat. Only rainbow trout are native to the park, and then only to the Merced River below about 4,000 feet in elevation. All other waters that contain fish were planted within the last 100 years up to 1991, when all fish planting stopped.

Fishing Licenses   Persons 16 years of age and older need a valid California fishing license to fish in Yosemite. You may purchase a license in Yosemite Valley, at Wawona, and El Portal year-round and at Tuolumne Meadows when open. Lake fishing is open year-round, but fishing in rivers and streams is open only from the last Saturday in April through November 15. An exception is Frog Creek, where the fishing season does not open until June 14. Parkwide limits are five trout per day, but no more than 10 fish in possession, except in the Merced River in Yosemite Valley. There, fishing for rainbow trout is catch-and-release only, and only artificial lures with barbless hooks are allowed. California fishing laws apply in the park, with some exceptions for special park regulations.

Regulations   You may fish only by hook and line. A rod or line must be closely attended. Chumming is illegal; so is possession of live or dead minnows, chubs, other bait fish, non-preserved fish eggs, and fish roe, or using any of these as bait. Do not fish from road bridges or designated swimming beaches. Digging or gathering any live bait such as worms, grubs, grasshoppers, hellgrammites, etc., is strictly forbidden. Certain waters may have special closures, seasons, or regulations, which are available at visitor centers or by writing to the park.

The National Park Service offers varied curriculum-based education programs. For elementary classes visiting the park for a day, a ranger-led **Parks as Classrooms** program emphasizes protection and preservation of the park's natural and cultural resources. Class size is limited, and the program is offered seasonally. There is also an **Environmental Living Program** at the Pioneer Yosemite History Center. Call the NPS Education Program at 375-9538 for more information, or visit its web site at http://www.nps.gov/yose/teach.htm.

Yosemite Institute   Hands-on outdoor education programs bring school classes to the park for week-long sessions. Led by authoritative instructors, sessions typically include day hikes and evening programs. Write to Yosemite Institute, P.O. Box 487, Yosemite, CA 95389, or telephone 379-9511.

Yosemite Association Field Seminars These adult and family outdoor educational programs, held throughout the year, last from one to eight days, and participants can camp for free or stay in park lodging at an additional cost. Topics include Sierra Nevada botany, forest ecology, birds, geology, Native American studies, photography, and art. Free catalogs are available at visitor centers, by calling 379-2321, or by writing to the Yosemite Association, P.O. Box 230, El Portal, CA 95318.

Research Library   Yosemite's Research Library in the Valley houses one of the National Park Service's most extensive and voluminous collections of park-based literature. It is open to the public; ask at the Valley Visitor Center about days and hours of operation.

Winter transforms Yosemite into a snowy wonderland of both scenic inspiration and winter sports. Ice and snow conditions that close many hiking trails open up ski touring, snowshoeing, and downhill skiing opportunities amidst breathtaking beauty. In the winter, precipitation above 4,000 to 5,000 feet in elevation usually falls as snow. Maximum snow depth occurs at 7,000 to 9,000 feet. In 1983, 211.5 inches of snow accumulated at Snow Flat, elevation 8,700 feet. Up to 90 percent of the Sierra's annual precipitation occurs between November and April, and most of this falls January through March.

Yosemite winter activities center around Crane Flat, Badger Pass Ski Area, and Yosemite Valley. See the *Yosemite Guide* for schedules of ranger-led winter activities and special programs. Roads to these areas are kept open but may be closed temporarily during or immediately after heavy storms. Ski and snowshoe trails are marked, and ski and topographic maps are available at visitor centers and ranger stations. Trails are marked for beginner, intermediate, and advanced levels of cross-country skiing. Trail lengths vary from one-half mile to loops of some 16 miles.

Crane Flat. Crane Flat offers cross-country skiing. **Badger Pass.** Located on the Glacier Point Road, Badger Pass Ski Area offers both downhill facilities and cross-country trails, equipment rentals, and downhill and Nordic ski schools. Rangers lead regularly scheduled snowshoe walks. At nearby Wawona you can walk through the Pioneer Yosemite History Center. The buildings—historic structures moved from elsewhere in the park for preservation and display—are closed in winter. However, informative signs make the center a self-guiding tour that imparts the flavor of Yosemite's history. **Yosemite Valley.** Nature walks, evening programs, films, and the Yosemite Museum form the core of winter program offerings in the Valley. Bicycle rentals, weather permitting, and two-hour bus tours are offered by the Yosemite Concession Services Corporation. Ice skating is available at the outdoor rink in Curry Village for part of the winter. The Valley Visitor Center is open daily; check the *Yosemite Guide* for hours of operation.

Overnight Accommodations   The Valley's Yosemite Lodge and Ahwahnee Hotel are open all winter. Its Curry Village cabins and tent cabins may close for part of the winter. Write or call the Yosemite Concession Services Corporation for current information and reservations. **Winter Camping.** At least one public campground in Yosemite Valley is kept open in winter except during and after exceptionally severe storms. The Wawona and Hodgdon Meadow campgrounds also remain open. Skiers and snowshoers may camp with a wilderness permit; check at a ranger station on restrictions for the Tuolumne and Mariposa groves, however. Reservations for the Ostrander Lake Ski Hut are handled by the Yosemite Association.

Overnight Wilderness Trips   All overnight trips require free wilderness permits. In addition, if you leave from the Badger Pass/Summit Meadow area you **must register** at the Badger Pass Ranger Station (A-frame) before any overnight trip. Permits are available at the Badger Pass Ranger Station, Valley Visitor Center, Wawona Ranger Station, and Big Oak Flat Information Station. Check your *Yosemite Guide* for current hours of operation. You must be prepared and equipped for emergencies, severe weather, and avalanche hazards.

Winter Driving Tips   Chains are often required on park roads that remain open in winter. Be especially alert for snowplows, stalled vehicles, rocks on road surfaces, and other unexpected situations. When roads are steep and slippery, gear down and pump your brakes. Do not lock your brakes. If your car goes into a skid, take your foot off the accelerator, pump your brakes lightly, and turn your steering wheel in the direction of the skid. Most serious accidents are caused by speed, alcohol, and crossing over the center line of the road.

Hypothermia Danger   Hypothermia is the lowering of the body's core temperature as a result of the body losing heat faster than it is produced. Potentially fatal, hypothermia can strike even in summer when wetness and wind compound effects of cool air. It takes more human lives yearly than does any other single outdoor hazard. Symptoms develop fast, and as they progress, you become less capable of realizing their significance. Hands and feet become numb as blood is diverted to vital organs. This results in uncontrollable shivering, fumbling, and drowsiness. Without proper treatment the next stages are stupor, collapse, and death. Stay dry, seek shelter from wind, avoid exhaustion, eat lots of high-energy foods, and wear a wool cap.

The Yosemite Association offers books, children's books, maps, posters, art prints, and other educational materials on Yosemite subjects for sale in the park and by mail. For a free bookstore catalog, write to Yosemite Association, P.O. Box 230, El Portal, CA 95318. Here is a select list of titles:

Arno, Stephen F. *Discovering Sierra Trees*. 1973.

Bunnell, Lafayette H. *Discovery of the Yosemite*. 1991.

Grater, Russell K. *Discovering Sierra Mammals*. 1978.

Harvey, H. T. et al. *The Sequoias of Yosemite National Park*. 1978.

Huber, N. King. *The Geologic Story of Yosemite National Park*. 1987.

La Pena, Frank, et al. *Legends of the Yosemite Miwok*. 1993.

Medley, Steven P. *The Complete Guidebook to Yosemite National Park-3rd edition*. 1997.

Muir, John. *The Wild Muir: Twenty-two of John Muir's Greatest Adventures*. 1994.

Neill, William, and Tim Palmer. *Yosemite: The Promise of Wildness*. 1996.

Russell, Carl P. *One Hundred Years in Yosemite*. 1993.

Schaffer, Jeffrey. *A Natural History Guide to Yosemite and its Trails*. 1995.

In addition to the guidelines and safety tips provided with descriptions of specific park activities in this Guide and Adviser section of your handbook, please heed the following guidelines and regulations.

Driving   Drive safely and defensively within posted speed limits. Do not stop in traffic lanes to look at scenery but be alert for drivers who do. Chains may be required on some park roads in winter (see Winter Activities). Park only in established turnouts and parking areas.

Rivers, Streams, and Waterfalls   Rivers, streams, and waterfalls can be treacherous at any time but especially when water levels are high. Approach cautiously and be alert for undermined banks and slippery rocks. Fast currents and cold water make a deadly combination. **Never swim above waterfalls or in swift water.**

Wildlife   All native animals are part of the natural systems protected in Yosemite National Park. Keep a respectful distance from wild animals so you do not disturb their natural routines. Feeding wildlife is dangerous, and it is illegal. Foodstuffs must be properly stored in vehicle trunks so bears cannot get them. In vehicles without trunks, cover food completely with a blanket, roll up the windows, and lock the doors. Use bear-proof food lockers where they are provided. Keep a clean camp; do not leave refuse or unattended food in camp anytime. Should you encounter a bear, keep your distance. If the bear approaches you, make loud noises and act aggressive to intimidate it. **Read and heed the Bear Warning on page 135.** If you are injured or your property is damaged by a bear, please report the incident to the nearest ranger station.

Pets   Pets must be leashed and under physical restraint at all times. They are not permitted on trails, in buildings, or in the backcountry. Pet regulations are enforced! The Yosemite Concession Services Corporation operates a boarding kennel in Yosemite Valley.

Hypothermia Danger   When body temperature lowers faster than the body can create heat, hypothermia sets in and can be fatal. This killer can strike even in summer; fatal hypothermia may develop in air temperatures of 50°F when it is wet and windy— or you are exhausted. **See Winter Activities for important information that can save your life.**

Fire Management   If you see smoke, it may be from a prescribed fire set by National Park Service rangers under proper conditions to help keep forests and meadows ecologically healthy and to restore natural conditions. It also might be from a prescribed natural fire—probably ignited by lightning— that is being allowed to burn. An early mistake in national parks management was to suppress **all** fires. Fire has been proven a vital process in keeping many natural ecosystems healthy. Occasional wildlands fires prevent fuel buildups that can lead to catastrophic forest fires. However, it remains imperative that you do nothing careless that could cause fires. If you see a fire you think may be a wildfire, please report it to a park ranger.

Devils Postpile National Monument and Sequoia and Kings Canyon National Parks Devils Postpile is a formation of columnar basalt on the Middle Fork of the San Joaquin River. Glaciers quarried away one side of the Postpile, exposing a sheer wall of columns 60 feet high. Fallen columns below lie jumbled like posts. Rainbow Falls here drops 101 feet. The John Muir Trail passes through the monument. A campground is open from about July 1 to mid-October. Devils Postpile lies west of U.S. 395 near Mammoth Lakes. It is closed in winter.

Sequoia and Kings Canyon National Parks can be reached by car only from the west, via Visalia, Fresno, and Bakersfield, California. Some trailheads can be reached from U.S. 395. These contiguous parks harbor myriad superlatives: spectacular canyons, the world's largest living thing, and the highest mountain in the United States outside Alaska. Canyons include the 3,000-foot-deep Kings Canyon. Mount Whitney stands at 14,495 feet in elevation. At 2,500 years old, the General Sherman Tree boasts both colossal size and antiquity. Giant sequoias, survivors of the last Ice Age, stand in a setting that fully matches their majesty. The John Muir Trail courses through both parks. For information about Devils Postpile and Sequoia and Kings Canyon write to Superintendent, Sequoia and Kings Canyon National Parks, Three Rivers, CA 93271.

Mono Lake Waters draining off Yosemite's steep eastern Sierra escarpment never reach the ocean. They naturally flow into Mono Lake, a Great Basin desert lake that has no outlet. Mono Lake's exotic tufa formations, built by mineral deposits from high-salinity lake waters, look like petrified forests from a distance. The lake and tufa are in the recently designated Mono Basin National Forest Scenic Area and Mono Lake Tufa State Reserve. The lake's future is uncertain because the Department of Water and Power of the City of Los Angeles diverts the water from its inlet streams southward via aqueduct for use in that sprawling metropolis. By 1928 Owens Lake, to the south, was sucked dry by Los Angeles diversions. It is now called Owens Dry Lake. For information contact the Mono Lake Visitor Center, P.O. Box 429, Lee Vining, CA 93541, 760-647-3044, or the Mammoth Ranger Station, P.O. Box 148, Mammoth Lakes, CA 93546, 760-934-2505.

The San Francisco Bay Area offers several National Park System sites. These are listed below with their information addresses: **Eugene O'Neill National Historic Site,** P.O. Box 280, Danville, CA 94526; **Fort Point National Historic Site,** P.O. Box 29333, Presidio of San Francisco, CA 94129; **Golden Gate National Recreation Area,** Fort Mason, San Francisco, CA 94123; **John Muir National Historic Site,** 4202 Alhambra Avenue, Martinez, CA 94553; **Muir Woods National Monument,** Mill Valley, CA 94941; **Point Reyes National Seashore,** Point Reyes, CA 94956; and **San Francisco Maritime National Historical Park,** Building E, Lower Fort Mason, San Francisco, CA 94123.

☆ GPO:1999—454-765/60511 Reprint 1999

National Park Service

The National Park Service expresses its appreciation to all those persons who made the preparation and production of this handbook possible. The Service also thanks the Yosemite Association for its financial support of this project. All photos and artwork not credited below come from the files of Yosemite National Park. Some materials from the park files are restricted against commercial reproduction.

The Bancroft Library, 50, 55, 65
Heinrich Berann 10-11
Henry B. Beville 48-49 reproductions
Steve Botti 94 Clarkia
Sonja Bullaty 68-69
David Cavagnaro 80, 93, 94 azalea and orchid, 95 orchid, 98 fox and deer
Vern Clevenger 108; 120 bivouac, some cracks, others vertical; 121 El Capitan
John Dawson 78-79, 84-89
Jeff Foott 95 poppies, 98 sheep
George Founds 100 bear
Jeff Gnass 6-7, 22-23, 32-33, 40, 70 right, 71 left
Annie Griffiths/DRK 96 falcon
Greg Harlin 104-105
Mary V. Hood 94 lily, 96 and 97 bluebirds, 98 mouse, 99 bobcats
Robert Hynes 76-77
Lewis Kemper 2-3, 26-27, 97 gull, 99 marmot, 119
Stephen J. Krasemann/DRK 97 young hawks, 98 raccoon, 99 mountain lion, badger and ringtail
Wayne Lankinen/DRK 96 woodpecker and owl, 99 black bear
Roger McGehee 94 violet, 95 spicebush and sky pilot, 96 blackbird, 97 owl
New York Public Library 51
Pat O'Hara 16, 19, 34, 35, 41, 44-46, 70 left, 71 right, 94 goldenrod
Stan Osolinsky 98 coyote
Peter Palmquist 53